An invaluable guide that tells you:

- How Drug Abusers Get Started
- How to Spot the Use of Drugs
- What to Do if You Learn that Your Youngster Is Sniffing Glue or Taking Cough Medicine
- What to Do if Your Youngster Is Exposed to Drugs
- What to Do if Your Youngster Is Smoking Marihuana
- What to Do if You Fear Your Youngster May Try LSD or Other Hallucinogens
- What to Do if Your Youngster Is Taking Pills
- What to Do if Your Youngster Is Taking Heroin or One of the Other Opiates

WHAT YOU CAN DO ABOUT
DRUGS AND YOUR CHILD
was originally published by
Hart Publishing Company, Inc.

What You Can Do about

DRUGS
and
YOUR CHILD

HERMAN W. LAND

With a Foreword by
HENRY BRILL, M.D.
DIRECTOR, PILGRIM STATE HOSPITAL
WEST BRENTWOOD, LONG ISLAND

PUBLISHED BY POCKET BOOKS NEW YORK

WHAT YOU CAN DO ABOUT DRUGS AND YOUR CHILD

Hart edition published June, 1969
Pocket Book edition published May, 1971

This *Pocket Book* edition includes every word
contained in the original, higher-priced edition. It is printed
from brand-new plates made from completely reset, clear, easy-to-read
type. *Pocket Book* editions are published by Pocket Books, a division
of Simon & Schuster, Inc., 630 Fifth Avenue, New York, N.Y. 10020.
Trademarks registered in the United States and other countries.

Standard Book Number: 671-78054-9.
Library of Congress Catalog Card Number: 68-29532.
Printed in the U.S.A.

Table of Contents

Preface

This is a book for the parent who is concerned about a potential or actual problem of teen-age drug abuse —a condition scientifically known as drug dependence.

Most of the available material in this field deals with the help required by the young victim. This book deals primarily with the needs of the parent, for the parent requires understanding and counsel during the soul-searching distress he faces during the process of diagnosis, treatment, and rehabilitation of a son or a daughter.

Experience with this new teen-age problem has built up rapidly during the last few years. Much expert consultation is to be had. Many treatment facilities are available; more are being opened. Yet the parent who faces an actual or a potential problem of this kind will often need assistance in determining exactly where to turn. What must he as a parent do? What may he expect during the course of treatment?

The book does not by any means pretend to be a substitute for consultation on specific cases, but the book does provide a detailed orientation which can be useful and reassuring at all stages of the problem. It may be said here that distraught parents are among the most touching and frequent by-products of teen-age drug abuse. Their concern is by no means unfounded, because the young and immature are particularly susceptible to the harmful effects of drug abuse, the most consistent one being that it deranges their education, often interrupting and even terminating it permanently.

In its present form, the disorder is new to our society. Never has there been such a widespread involvement with drugs among young people. Only a few years ago it was virtually unknown for teenagers to take drugs for pleasure—aside from cases among the emotionally disturbed and among those in the poorest areas of some large cities. Today, more than a quarter of the freshman classes of many colleges freely state that they have taken drugs for pleasure on one or more occasions, and some two to five percent of college students appear to be seriously involved. For the most part, the reasons for this vast amount of drug taking are not related to social stress, nor to clearly defined mental or emotional disorders. Many of the cases arise among boys and girls who were reared in highly favored sectors of our society, and most of the drug takers are not obviously maladjusted.

Parental concern is intensified by another new element in the situation. Youth is no longer guilty or apologetic about drug abuse. On the contrary, youth often vigorously defends drug taking in principle even though the protagonist himself may not seriously or may not be at all involved at the time. For parents who face such situations, this book provides useful information.

As in many other forms of risk taking, catastrophe is the exception and not the rule. Many are "getting away with it." Yet drug taking is by no means harmless and catastrophes do occur. Some adverse reactions are clear cut and even spectacular. Here we may include acute attacks of mental disorder with hallucinations, delusions, episodes of unpredictable or violent behavior, and medical complications which are especially frequent when the drugs are taken by injection.

Other adverse reactions likewise insidious, are no less significant and perhaps far more frequent. Here we may include the reactions of young persons who, following the injunction of certain cultists, just "turn on and drop out." They lose interest in work and studies, suffer a decline of general energy, abolish all schedules, repeal the laws of hygiene, and withdraw into a strange dream world where the only reality is the unreality of the drug experience. This is a frightening prospect for any parent.

Private psychiatric hospitals have been admitting increasing numbers of teen-aged drug users since the early 1960's, so many that their capacity to handle such cases has long since been reached. It is now often difficult to arrange for an admission of this type. Public psychiatric facilities, too, have been experiencing an influx of this new type of case.

Incidentally, the problem is not purely an American one; similar reports have been coming from abroad, especially from Britain, the Scandinavian countries, and surprisingly enough from Japan, where drug abuse was virtually unknown before World War II.

Drug abuse aggravates the effects of more traditional teen-age problems, such as automobile accidents, alcohol misuse, sexual delinquency, money problems, educational failure, and school drop-out.

Most parents feel that they have devoted a lifetime to providing for the material needs of their child; it is a painful thought to such a parent that all this effort may not have been enough; that in spite of financial security, a good home, and virtually unlimited educational opportunities, his child may still fall prey to a curse which hardly existed only a few years ago.

It is then not surprising that parents avidly seek information as to what they can or should do in relation to this problem. At every public meeting where drugs are the subject of discussion, parents ask many questions and many then wait till after the close of the meeting to ask still more. The major themes are, "What can I do if——?" "How can I tell?" "Where can I get help?"

Final answers are not always to be expected—even from experts. Still less from a general discussion in a book. Yet each person who encounters such a problem must go through the same painful process of evaluating the situation, reading about it, locating experts in the field, consulting with such experts, and if need be, working with them in the subsequent course of treatment. Just developing an orientation—if thoroughly done—involves a vast amount of personal effort, more than the average person has time and energy for.

It is here that Mr. Land has done a major service. He has interviewed all kinds of persons with experience in the field: psychiatrists, social workers, ex-addicts, law-enforcement officials, judges, workers in voluntary agencies, and parents. He has gone through all of the steps. He has reduced his experiences to a single volume which provides an interpretation of the literature. The emphasis is always on *what is of use to the parent seeking help.*

Finally, the book includes an appendix with names and addresses of agencies to which one may turn. Included also is a description of how one may use local, state, and national specialized agencies such as the New York State Narcotic Addiction Control Commission.

The book repeatedly emphasizes that where there seems to be a drug problem, the situation requires realistic attitudes. The situation can be made much worse by panic, by confusion, by exaggeration, by lack of understanding, by indecisiveness and by uncritical acceptance of prevalent notions.

Here, too, the book makes a useful contribution. The author deals effectively with a series of misconceptions. He disposes of the myth of the pusher as a cause of drug abuse; and in its stead, describes the real causes as social contagion and the example of friends. He correctly points out that "the drug fiend" and the horrible physical changes he is supposed to undergo are myths; and in their place, he describes a drug-dependent youth as a sick personality. Mythical also is the hopeless outlook on addiction; for even the most serious cases can and do recover, although the treatment is long and arduous both for the youth and for his parent.

Finally, the important distinction between experimentation with drugs and full involvement is put into clear perspective. So, too, are the important differences among drugs.

Much of the discussion is about drug dependence generally. This is valid because the teen-age problem tends to be *multiple* drug use rather than exclusive concentration on one substance. A bibliography of references tells where more detailed and the difficult aspects of the question may be researched.

The material in this book will be of interest not only to worried parents, but to teachers, advisors, and group leaders. The material is factual, is valid, is succinct, and is presented in laymen's language. The author directs himself consistently to the concerned parent, and offers advice as to what should be said, and what should not be said, and the manner of the approach. Even the wording of a conversation is suggested, as in the instance where parents are obliged to inform other parents that both boys may be involved with drugs.

In a word, this book promises to meet a practical need.

Henry Brill, M.D.

Author's Foreword

This book is written for parents, by a parent. It was conceived not long ago when I was searching libraries and book stores for material that would help me understand the basics of what was becoming prominent in the news: drug abuse. In my own suburban county just outside New York City, whispers were being heard about the drug usage that was beginning to show up in the high schools. Several of us with teenage children began to be concerned. We knew that heroin and marihuana were somehow involved with it all, and we had visions of "pushers" seducing gullible youngsters. When I stopped to think about the subject seriously, I realized that in reality I knew very little about it, and so I set about to learn something.

I found technical monographs, learned books by scholars, researchers and physicians, along with colorful and sensational press and magazine accounts. Little was directed to me as a parent, giving me commonsense advice on how to think and deal with the question. Nowhere was there anything which dealt with the inner fears of parents, the question of a parent's relationship to his child, or what to say to friends and neighbors. Nowhere could I find out how a parent should come to grips with his sense of shame. Should he preserve secrecy? Where could he go for help? As I delved into the technical material, I became convinced that a book was necessary.

Thus began a long investigation which brought me into direct touch with experts, in medicine, psychiatry, social work and the law, with addicts and ex-addicts and their families, with ministers, with county, state and federal officials, probation officers, and assistant district attorneys. I studied volumes and monographs and reports by the yard. Curiously, despite the fierce disputes in which the experts engaged over theories of treatment and social control, there turned out to be surprisingly little disagreement about the basic things parents should do.

It is these basics which this volume deals with. It serves as a bridge between the expert and the parent. What appears in these pages is the distilled advice of some of the outstanding authorities in the country.

I, myself, make no claim to be an expert, nor do I espouse one course of treatment over another. When the experts are at odds, it is foolish—perhaps even dangerous—for the layman to urge one or another medical approach. The book concentrates on the role of the parent in this melancholy situation: how you should handle yourself, your spouse and your child through the trying days. In many ways, this is the most difficult part of the whole problem. Indeed, it is often the inability of the parent to cope with the fundamental family relationships that is the root of the trouble that causes drug addiction.

I have attempted to deal in straightforward fashion with painful subjects, such as the difficulty parents have in accepting the truth when their own child is involved, and the dangerous paralysis of will that so frequently results. The picture of the addict is fully drawn, uncompromisingly, so that you may know what you are really dealing with, and just why addiction is such a curse. At the same time, I have tried to cut through the miasma of misinformation that has so long made rational approach to the problem by laymen almost impossible. You will see how drug addiction begins; you will understand something of how to spot the trouble; you will be given pointers on what steps to take, from talking to your child to forcing a medical examination when the chips are down. You will also find information on where to go for information and help in your state.

Where possible, I have quoted directly from my interviews. In many instances, anonymity was requested. Every effort has been made to present the expert's point of view with accuracy.

To list all of those who have made contributions to this volume is virtually impossible. Space permits only the following expressions of gratitude:

To Dr. Henry Brill, Vice Chairman, New York State Narcotic Addiction Control Commission and Director of Pilgrim State Hospital; Dr. Daniel Casriel, Medical Director, Daytop Village; David Deutsch, Director, Daytop Village; Dr. Mark Kenyon, Director, Nassau County Medical Society; Dr. Jerome Levine, Assistant Chief, Psychopharmacology Branch, National Institute of Mental Health; Dr. Pat Hughes, The Center for Studies of Narcotic and Drug Abuse, National Institute of Mental Health; Irving Gaffney, Federal Bureau of Narcotics; Miss Edith Yungblut, Community Action Program of the Office of Economic Opportunity; Leon Brill, formerly Director Washington Heights Demonstration Center, Director New Jersey Department of Community Affairs; Dr. Stoyan Stematovich, Department of Mental Hygiene, New York State; Percy Mason, psychiatrist; Seymour

Fiddle, research sociologist, Exodus House; Dr. Irwin
Gould, Director narcotics program, Post-Graduate
Center, N.Y.; Drs. Pinney and Michaels, Brooklyn-
Cumberland Medical Center; Louis J. Milone, Pro-
bation Director, Nassau County, N.Y.; probation
officers Hilton, Beckerman and Barnett of New York
City; Dr. Robert Simon, Director of Psychiatry,
Community Mental Health Services, Westchester
County; David Feldstein, Westchester County Mental
Health Board; Dr. Jack Goldman, 1st Deputy Com-
missioner of Health for Westchester County; John
Jay, Sheriff, Westchester County; Theodore Levine,
school counselor; Frank Boxwill, Sol Froshnider,
school psychologists; Robert Slawson, Director,
Southwest Fairfield Experimental Program; Panetta
Taylor, narcotics program, Yonkers; Lars Nyman,
social worker, Quakers; Eliot Elaseph, social worker;
Dr. Efren Ramirez, Director, Office of the Coordi-
nator of Addiction Programs, New York City; Irving
Lang, General Counsel, New York State Narcotic
Addiction Control Commission; Murray Itzkowitz,
Jewish Board of Guardians; Leonard Singer, Samari-
tan Halfway House; Nathan Zucker, The Family
Council on Narcotics; Elizabeth Goddard, welfare
worker; Father Damian Pitcaithly, Astoria Health
Center; The Reverend David Wilkinson, Director,
Teen Challenge; The Reverend James Allen, Chris-
tian Reformed Church; The Reverend Lynn Hege-
mann, Director, Exodus House; The Reverend
Edward Brown, Lower East Side Information and
Youth Center; George Danelly and Henry Ablesser,
Youth Counseling Service, District Attorney, New
York County; Dr. S. B. Sells, Professor and Director,
Institute of Behavioral Research, Texas Christian

University, who made available lists of facilities being compiled for the National Institute of Mental Health.

Very personal and deeply felt thanks to Joseph Stone, Assistant District Attorney, New York County, a dedicated public servant and a dear friend for his counsel, aid and generous cooperation; to Leon Morse, my associate and research aide, for his energy, his devotion to the project, and his iron legs, for the many arguments we have enjoyed, and for his amazing ability to deliver the goods under pressure; to my daughter Mady, whose young presence was the cause of it all, and who spent long hours transcribing tape interviews and reports and preparing the endless cards and lists and who did so much typing and retyping; and to my wife Dorothy, who somehow managed to survive while the papers piled up and covered the house and lights burned into the night, living proof that it is possible to live though wed to an author.

What You Can Do
about
DRUGS
and
YOUR CHILD

1: Cause for Alarm

There's something different about your adolescent son's behavior:

Normally, he's a happy youngster, doing pretty well in school, busy with sports and other extra-curricular activities. Suddenly, he seems to have lost interest. He's stopped doing his homework, dropped out of sports, and has been staying away from school more frequently than he should. He's even wondering out loud whether it makes any sense to bother with finishing high school.

Or, it was just a short time ago that he developed an intense interest in girls, natural in a healthy teenage boy. But now he is indifferent to girls without being able to explain why.

Or, you notice the secret telephone calls, the endless locked-door chats with his buddy, his withdrawal from most of his former friends. There are new friends, different from the old, a little wilder, odder, more rebellious and daring.

Or, he's peevish these days, suddenly breaking out with angry remarks when he's never been that way. And he stays alone in the bathroom or bedroom for long periods.

Are these changes just part of growing up? Adolescence, after all, is filled with change, sometimes of a pretty bewildering kind. Why suppose that he had been taking drugs? The answer, of course, is that you shouldn't. But perhaps there are some other signs, even more alarming:

> *The healthy look is gone from his face. His appearance, never the neatest, is now slovenly. He yawns frequently, even in the middle of the day when he should be raring to go. His sense of timing sometimes seems to be off, and you've seen him stagger as if he were drunk, although there's no smell of alcohol on his breath. There's very little doubt left when you find hidden in his room a little box of pills, tablets, or capsules.*

But don't jump to the conclusion that your son is an addict. He may be just experimenting; just at the beginning. You are lucky if you move at this early stage, for there still is a chance to head off the worst as long as you inform yourself of the facts about drug abuse and take some firm intelligent steps. If your youngster is only experimenting, addiction may very well be avoided.

To start with, it will probably be necessary for you to change some of your attitudes, because the chances are that like most Americans, you find the whole subject frightening. You probably have an image in your mind of the "dope fiend" that fills you with disgust and revulsion. You link him with crime and the sordid life of the underworld. The idea of your child becoming or being a "dope fiend" causes your insides to knot with horror, and all at once there comes to mind the terrible picture of the addict as described in lurid newspaper and magazine stories and "scare" pamphlets puts out by well-meaning organizations. A description of the drug addict, which appeared in a Supreme Court decision a few years ago, is typical:

"To be a confirmed drug addict is to be one of the walking dead . . . the teeth have rotted out, the appetite is lost and the stomach and intestines don't function properly. The gall bladder becomes inflamed, eyes and skin turn a bilious yellow; in some cases membranes of the nose turn a flaming red; the partition separating the nostrils is eaten away—breathing is difficult. Oxygen in the blood decreases; bronchitis and tuberculosis develop. Sex organs become affected. Veins collapse and livid purplish scars remain. Boils and abscesses plague the skin; gnawing pain racks the body. Nerves snap; vicious twitching develops. Imaginary and fantastic fears blight the mind and sometimes complete insanity results. Oftentimes, too, death comes—much too early in life. . . . Such is the torment of being a drug addict; such is the plague of being one of the walking dead."

There is one trouble with this picture. It just isn't so. For years authorities on the subject have pointed out that such descriptions are vast exaggerations. Still, the myth persists. The trouble is, that it prevents people from dealing with addiction as it really is—an illness, a difficult chronic illness. It is very hard to take sensible steps, when instead of a sick person, you have in your mind the image of a monster.

There is another kind of damage such descriptions do. Instead of discouraging narcotics abuse, they can actually promote it. Dr. Henry Brill, Director of Pilgrim State Hospital in Brentwood, New York, and Vice-Chairman of the New York State Narcotics Control Commission, says: "The false horror stories have a tendency to defeat themselves when the kid sees an addict who doesn't have yellow skin or teeth.

He's likely to interpret this to mean that there is an immunity and that people can get away with using drugs. I have talked to many addicts who are highly amused at these fantastic, embroidered stories. They laugh at them. They know these stories are not true."

Furthermore, Dr. Brill points out, there is the danger that the horror stories will actually attract the people they are trying to warn off. "Danger and forbidden fruit tend to attract all people to a certain extent. Some addicts have told me that they were attracted to narcotics by the stories." In one case, an addict reported that he had read a series in a newspaper which graphically portrayed the horrors of addiction and decided: "This is for me."

In other words, there is much misinformation about the subject of narcotics and addiction, and before the parent can take the necessary action, he must clear his mind of false, misleading, and often dangerous ideas. Otherwise, he will either be paralyzed and do nothing, which would be disastrous, or do the wrong thing out of hysteria and revulsion, which would be equally as bad.

THE NATURE OF DRUG ADDICTION

The first and most important thing to understand about drug addiction is that you are dealing with *a sick way of life*—

—not criminality;
—not immorality;
—not stubborn disobedience.

These things are involved, yes. They are part of the overall problem of addiction, but they are not at its core. The core is an *illness,* a difficult, chronic illness that is not completely understood.*

This means that you cannot simply depend on the addict's "will power" to help him overcome his problem. It is as though some terribly vicious virus had entered into his system, rendering him incapable of normal behavior. Therefore it is pointless to accuse a young person of doing something terrible, of breaking the law, of stupidly disobeying his parents, of being immoral, of bringing disgrace to the family, of letting you down. These things may in some cases be true—but they are irrelevant. Hammering away at such accusations will accomplish nothing. Indeed, you will probably make things worse and stimulate your youngster to fight you harder and go even more deeply into his addiction.

The parent must be warned that the greatest obstacles to the sensible handling of a drug situation involving his own child, are the prejudices and fears he is in all likelihood harboring. This point cannot be over-emphasized. When confronted by the dreadful truth, the parent must steel himself and try as hard as he can to adopt the attitude that he is dealing with a *disease.* He must realize however strange, surprising, distasteful, or even shocking his child's behavior may turn out to be, *this behavior must be regarded as a natural and almost inevitable aspect of the disease.*

Obviously, no parent can be expected to be completely detached when he sees his child stealing, lying, cheating, withdrawing from the world, running around with drug-users, and wasting his life away.

---

* Technically speaking, addiction is not considered a *disease,* but rather a *condition, a sick way of life;* however, for all practical purposes, it should be approached as though it were a disease.

But unless he is capable of achieving *some* detachment, unless he can learn to look at all of these things as symptoms of the disease itself, unless, in other words, he recognizes that this is the kind of disease addiction is, he will not be able to deal with it.

You may be wondering: "stealing," "cheating"? Is this what we're talking about? Weren't we talking about the effects of drugs on the victim, the things it does to the body, and the tortures the victim is subjected to? Well, once again, here is the problem of too much misinformation. The real damage caused by drug abuse is not so much to the body of the victim, as it is to his personality, his spirit.

Just why this is so becomes clear when we examine the process of addiction. Drug abuse ordinarily stems from a desire to escape from problems. An adolescent boy, for example, takes a shot of heroin and finds he feels better about his problems. The matters that were "bugging" him don't seem very troublesome or worth being concerned with. He feels at peace with himself and the world. In this state of euphoria he has the illusion that he's now handling things pretty well.

Nothing terrible seems to have happened; in fact, it all appears rather pleasant and harmless although there are cases where this first shot is an unpleasant experience. So the young man decides to try it again, and then again.

After a couple of weeks of this, curious things begin to happen. In the first place, whatever momentary pleasure he may have gotten out of the shots seems to be gone. The glamour, if there was any, the excitement of doing the illegal and dangerous, has gone—and in such a short time! Still, he finds himself seeking out more heroin and waiting impatiently to take that next shot. A mysterious thing is going on in his body that is still not fully understood by doctors. But that it *is* going on, is the fact and the heart of the problem.

The boy is building up what medicine terms "tolerance." At the start, one shot does the job. Very, very quickly, the boy finds that this amount is not enough. He needs twice the amount of heroin to achieve the same lift he got from the first shot. A very short time later, he needs three times the amount. It isn't very long before he goes to four, five, six, seven, eight, nine, ten times the original dose. The amount of heroin a fully developed addict can consume without self-destruction often would kill a person who took that amount for the first time.

By this time the user has also developed a physical dependence on the drug. As soon as the heroin starts to wear off he becomes restless and irritable, his eyes run, he yawns, he sweats, his temperature goes up, his blood pressure rises, he vomits, he has diarrhea—the well-known "withdrawal" symptoms. A change has taken place in his nervous system and body cells. Now he literally *needs* the drug. His entire being is directed toward only one desperate end: to get rid of these terrible feelings and pains. And there is only one way he knows how to do this—another shot of heroin.

Now it is clear what a self-defeating and self-destructive, vicious process this has to be. After a very brief respite from his troubles, he starts suffering varying degrees of discomfort as the withdrawal symptoms begin to appear. Naturally he anticipates the worst, and begins to seek relief before the agony really begins. That shot, too, soon wears off, and he starts his hunt to avoid his withdrawal troubles all over again. Now he needs more heroin more frequently. There seems to be no end to the cycle. Soon after he gives himself the shot and relaxes, the body begins to send out its urgent messages. By this time he is shooting the drug into himself four or five times a day.

He has to have it! But possession of heroin for either use or sale is illegal, punishable by long imprisonment. It is therefore distrubuted by the underworld, and the price is high—five to ten dollars an ounce. He may have to spend as much as $40.00 a day—$280.00 a week. Only a very wealthy person can afford this; all others must get the money some other way.

And so the addict steals. He steals from department stores, neighborhood retail shops. He turns burglar, hunting for money or anything he can carry away to pawn or sell—jewelry, television sets, typewriters, clothing, furniture. He will steal his own family's personal belongings and most cherished treasures, and in time, if not stopped, will empty the house, so great is his compulsion.

There are cases of addicts stealing even from the district attorney's office and from the very court where their fate is being decided. Some addicts become "pushers" themselves, narcotic peddlers who raise the money to feed their own habit by selling drugs to others. Females usually turn to prostitution.

Addicts become psychologically dependent on the drug. This lasts for a long, long time after the physical dependence has been cured. Few youngsters, or adults, are prepared to accept the idea that they can become *psychologically hooked* on a drug. It seems a bizarre notion, and insubstantial. Yet it is the most desperate part of addiction.

It is, surprisingly, easy enough to "cure" an addict

in a physical sense. This can be often accomplished for heroin in a matter of seventy-two hours, although sometimes, the "detoxification" can take up to five, six or even seven days. And while there is considerable discomfort for the patient, there are rarely the wild, violent, convulsive, writhing-on-the-floor-in-agony symptoms commonly thought to be part of the usual withdrawal. In many cases, addicts will tell you, withdrawal is not very much worse than a severe cold.

It is quite different on the emotional and mental level, for the heroin user will leave the hospital freed of the drug, his body cleansed, yet as a rule will immediately head for a heroin supplier. This is the true tragedy of addiction.

FROM MEDICINE TO MENACE

Although heroin is the narcotic we usually think of in connection with addiction, the barbiturates in several ways actually represent a far more serious problem. These are the drugs we are so familiar with as tranquilizers and sleeping pills: phenobarbital, luminal, nembutal, seconal, barbital, pentothal. Taken when and as prescribed by a doctor, the barbiturate is a perfectly good and acceptable item in our society. There is nothing against the law in having tranquilizers or sleeping pills in the home or in using them. Millions are sold legally every year. But when used in excess, they can be very harmful. They are just as addicting as heroin and much more dangerous because of what can happen when there is a sudden withdrawal.

Barbiturate abusers do not take those pills to produce sleep or relax but to become intoxicated, and they look very much like someone who is drunk. According to Dr. Edward R. Bloomquist of the University of Southern California, the person "high" on barbiturates "staggers, has slurred speech, and finds it hard to perform coordinated activities. He acts as if he were drunk and, unfortunately, is often mistaken as a drunk by traffic officers." His sense of time gets mixed up, he doesn't quite know what is happening or how many pills he has taken. He begins to think that a few more will make him feel "higher," and this all too frequently leads to a fatal overdose.

When addiction occurs, says Dr. Bloomquist, it "always causes a marked social and emotional deterioration. Many of the addicts neglect themselves. Their nutrition suffers. They let themselves go. . . . They are rejected by friends and family. They lose their jobs. Their associates refuse to tolerate their erratic behavior and frequently reject them. . . . They often smoke in bed and start serious fires." Conceivably they may even commit crimes and not remember them. In short, observes Dr. Bloomquist, they greatly resemble the chronic alcoholic with whom they share many similar emotional problems.

The barbiturate user builds up a tolerance and dependence in the same way a heroin user does. Moreover, like a heroin victim, he will go to whatever lengths necessary to get the drug.

"A barbiturate addiction," writes Dr. Marie Nyswander in her book The Drug Addict as Patient, "builds up in easy stages:

"The patient usually begins with a prescribed dosage. Instead of resting in bed until the drug works, he sits up and reads until it 'knocks him out.' While reading, a drowsy euphoria slowly envelops him, replacing his anxiety with a sense of well being. When he subsequently experiences anxiety or tension, . . . he is likely to recall the effect of sleeping pills and take one during the daytime, with *no intention of sleeping*. This marks the second step in his addiction. Within a relatively short time he will be taking four grains a day. With the building up of tolerance comes the usual need of ever-increasing doses and it is not unusual to find an addict taking fifteen to thirty grains a day of a barbiturate." Sudden withdrawal results in severe mental confusion, delirium, or even death.

Today many young people who have trouble sleeping or falling asleep pester their parents for sleeping pills. To oblige is very foolish and dangerous. No matter how tempted you may be to get your teenager to bed at a reasonable hour, you are courting serious trouble if you give him sleeping pills or tranquilizers, even those you have reason to believe are not very powerful. It's so easy to start a habit.

When you remember that the psychological dependence on narcotics remains long after the strictly physical symptoms have gone, it is not surprising that one can become dependent upon drugs that do not cause a physical addiction. This is the case, for example, with the easily obtainable and often misused "pep" pill—amphetamine, which is usually sold under the trade names Benzedrine and Dexedrine.

To the college student, and more recently to many a high school student, amphetamine seems an old and reliable friend, whose main purpose is to help him stay awake long enough to cram successfully for the exam that he will have to face in the morning. Truck drivers depend on it to keep them from falling asleep at the wheel on long overnight drives. For years physicians have been employing it to treat a variety of mental diseases, particularly of the milder kinds, and to help in what are termed "mood" disturbances. It is also used to help overweight patients and for treatment of narcolepsy, Parkinson's Disease, and other ailments.

Again, it should be noted that we are talking about abuse, not sensible use as directed by a physician. The same feeling of alertness or well-being that helps a patient suffering from, say, sleeping sickness, can be the source of the greatest danger.

When taken in excess, amphetamine produces a form of intoxication. The user becomes agitated, restless, and talkative. Irritability, argumentativeness, and combativeness are not uncommon. His skin becomes flushed, he perspires freely, the pupils of his eyes dilate, his blood pressure rises, his reflexes become superactive, and he startles very easily. Sometimes his hands shake, and he may have paranoid delusions or hallucinations. For example, he may think that he is being followed by enemies, or that he hears voices talking about him. If an overdose is taken, severe illness or even death can result.

While amphetamine does not produce the physical dependence or withdrawal problems that heroin and sleeping pills can cause, excessive use of it often brings about a mental and emotional dependence, which is every bit as serious. The user begins to "need" the drug in order to get through the day. Without it he feels drained and miserable; he seems to lack the energy to do his work and face his problems. Moreover, because amphetamine is a stimulant, a person who takes it cannot sleep at night, so often he takes sleeping pills to counteract the effect of the "pep" pills. The result is that sooner or later he winds up an addict in the full sense of the word.

2: How Drug Abusers
Get Started

Youngsters are often introduced to the use of drugs at the conventional teen-age party when there is no supervision by adults. Usually, they begin by smoking marihuana. Some—not many, but some—go on to try other drugs and wind up using heroin, barbiturates, cocaine, or opium.

Here is how one middle-class, suburban girl describes her first exposure to marihuana to the author:

"There were two new boys at the party. They were kind of superior to everybody in the way they acted. One of them took a small brown envelope out of his pocket and asked us if we'd ever seen what was inside. He passed it around. The envelope contained what looked like blackish powder. He said it was marihuana. I didn't really know what marihuana was. Everybody was curious, but that was all. Nothing else happened."

Nothing happened, except that a group of sixteen and seventeen year old boys and girls were now aware of a new substance in their lives and began to talk about it. Eventually some of them tried it.

Another girl reported:

"I was with my girl-friend in——[a teenage dance hangout]. One of the musicians was talking with us. He seemed a little tipsy. He asked us if we had ever

13

used marihuana. Naturally, we hadn't. He offered us some. My friend was angry and moved away. But he and I talked. We were having a good time. I know I shouldn't have, but I suppose it was the atmosphere, the music, the beer—anyway, I decided to try one."

Very often the youngster assumes that it must be all right, since his friends are doing it. A boy from a big-city slum, who had been smoking marihuana describes his introduction to heroin:

"I was at a party. Everybody was having a good time. I wanted to be one of the crowd. I thought, if it didn't hurt them, it wouldn't hurt me. That started the ball rolling. They were sniffing [heroin] at that time. Two or three pulled out a few caps, and said 'Here if you want to, try.' I accepted. They just gave it to me."[1]

It may occur as casually as this, in a typical city scene:

"I guess it was sort of a lark. At this time, anyway, we were all of us off on a kick. I was sixteen years old exactly, and I was walking with a friend on Henry Street and he asked me, 'Have you ever smoked pot before?' I didn't know what pot was, and I had to ask him, so he told me it was marihuana and I almost fell with shock. But then he talked about it, and he explained to me it was nothing to worry about, and three days later I was smoking my first weed. Three months afterward, I was snorting heroin."[2]

Note that in every case it was a friend or acquaintance who introduced the youngster to the illicit drug.

[1] Isidor Chein, Donald L. Gerard, Robert S. Lee, and Eva Rosenfeld, *The Road to H, Narcotics, Delinquency and Social Policy;* Basic Books, 1964.

[2] Jeremy Larner and Ralph Tefferteller, *The Addict in the Street;* Grove Press, 1964.

Where is the much-talked-of "pusher" in all this? He's around, but not where your child can see him. Researchers and police report that drug abuse spreads from abuser to abuser, that the figure of the lurking adult preying on the unsuspecting youngsters is largely myth. It is a "seller's market," they say. Illegal drug peddlers have all the customers they can handle, and they don't need to take the risk involved in enticing children to try their wares. The boy or girl seeks out the supplier, and not the other way around.

WHY THEY ARE FOOLING WITH DRUGS

You must always keep in mind that there is a great difference between *experimentation* and *addiction*. During their adolescence youngsters are prone to try forbidden fruits, to sample what the world has to offer. It is a time of reaching out, of adventurous experimentation. And because so many young people today can get about easily and have money to spend they are exposed to a greater variety of temptations than were preceding generations.

Most students of the narcotics problem hold that teenage experimentation with drugs is understandable, considering our fast-moving, rapidly-changing world clouded over by the unrelieved threat of war. They argue that the youngsters are expressing their resentment of materialism and hypocrisy, of the Cold War, the war in Vietnam, of the injustices in our society. Experimentation with drugs they view as a form of rebellion and an assertion of individuality in a world trying to make the youngsters conform.

In big-city slums, especially areas where oppressed minorities live, ordinary youthful adventurousness and resentment are often accompanied by a desire to escape from intolerable poverty; a feeling of despair arises from the lack of opportunity. How this sense of hopelessness affects a young person is reported in a study of addiction among adolescents in New York, *The Road to H.* The authors write of "an attitude of surrender, a mood of 'What difference does it make anyhow?' When one is in this mood, hardly any argument against heroin use is convincing, and most tend to be rejected outright. The point of greatest danger seems to be right here. . . . When one is in a mood of hopelessness and futility . . . the . . . effects of the drug are directly relevant, they provide a chemical balm to a sorely depressed spirit."

But, as the book points out, not every one in the deprived areas tries drugs. In fact, even in the worst streets, the places where the highest percentage of addiction is found, only a small percentage of youngsters get involved. How come? Since the conditions are roughly the same for most of the adolescents living there, why do some seek out drugs and others shun them?

The answer given by psychiatrically-minded experts is that a youngster fools with drugs because he, or she is having problems in growing up. For some reason the boy or girl cannot cope with them as well as others do, and drugs provide an escape. Needless to say, adolescents in families of every income level have problems, and so—according to this interpretation—drug taking is the youngster's way of avoiding and postponing the responsibilities of adulthood.

A boy who gets involved may be too dependent on his mother, not able to identify himself with a strong father-figure, and be filled with sexual anxieties. Girls, presumably, have a less difficult time in identifying with their mothers as the family function is so much a part of being a female. However, they may be drawn to drugs because of sexual anxieties or feelings of inadequacy, especially if they are in a group where using drugs is thought to be sophisticated and they lack the self-assurance to resist. For these reasons many thoughtful students of the drug problem consider experimentation to be an indication of what psychiatrists call personality or character disorders.

WILL HE EXPERIMENT?

Whatever the reasons are that youngsters experiment with drugs, it is very possible that at one time or another yours will be tempted to do so. For the illicit use of drugs in one form or another is very widespread.

The Federal Narcotics Bureau estimates that there are approximately 60,000 heroin addicts in the United States. But this figure is based on known arrests only and does not, and cannot, take into account the "hidden" users who have never been arrested.

The New York State Narcotic Addiction Control Commission estimated that as of May, 1968, there were 32,000 addicts in that state alone, approximately half the national total. Of the state total, about half were in New York City. Some estimates are considerably higher. Dr. Efrim Ramirez, New York City Narcotics Coordinator, has based his entire program on the assumption that there may be as many as 100,000 addicts within the city's border.

Statistics on the number of people who use barbiturates and amphetamine for non-medical purposes virtually do not exist, though one hears estimates ranging from the hundreds of thousands to millions. Some experts believe that as many as a million people smoke marihuana occasionally or frequently. One authority reported to the author that 30 percent of the entering freshmen of several Eastern colleges have already had some drug experience prior to entering. LSD usage has increased in the late sixties, and the sniffing of glue and other inhalants and drinking of cough medicine are extensive among children in their early teens.

You probably have most cause for concern if you live in New York, Chicago, Los Angeles, Detroit, or Washington, which, according to the Federal Bureau of Narcotics, account for about three-fourths of the country's heroin addicts. Heroin is the drug most often used among the economically deprived of these big cities and others. Marihuana usage, too, is considerable. As you go up the economic scale and out into the suburbs, heroin usage tends to decrease and consumption of marihuana, sleeping and pep pills tends to go up. By 1968, however, it had begun to appear that the usage of heroin was beginning to rise in the suburbs.

But it no longer is any guarantee of safety that you live in one of the so-called drug-free states, such as North Dakota, Alaska, or Utah. Young people travel more than you did at their age and sooner or later will probably go to an infected area. This could happen, for example, at a resort. Miami Beach Chief of Police Rocky Pomerance reports:

"During the height of the tourist influx, trafficking in all drug classifications will at least double or triple. The transient seller will bring his own supply of drugs for sale to the local residents, while enjoying his stay here throughout the winter season. His home town contacts will replenish his supply via the mails or any other means of conveyance. Every year it is as if our town has been invaded by a gang of Typhoid Marys!"[3]

Because drug experimentation is common in many colleges, high school students are subject to additional hazards. A school administrator reports that during the college vacation periods, when the students return to their homes, there is a sudden rise in marihuana and barbiturate usage among the high school pupils.

Since your youngster may well be exposed to the drug threat, it is quite possible that he will experiment. Of course, statistics on this are non-existent, but the chances are better than even, especially if you live in or near a big city. The question is, just how dangerous is experimentation?

WILL HE WIND UP AN ADDICT?

Experimentation does not necessarily lead to addiction. It is just not true to say that one or even a few tries of a habit-forming drug will "hook" the youngster. But psychiatrists estimate that up to one fourth of the American population may be "overtly" disturbed, that is, mentally or emotionally ill to the point where some treatment is already required. They also point out that if you add the mild neuroses and the disturbances in individual and family life caused by modern pressures, the figure may go up considerably

[3] International Narcotic Enforcement Officers Association, *6th Annual Conference Report*, Sept. 26–Oct. 1, 1965.

above 50 percent. Therefore, many youngsters have a psychological inclination toward the drug habit and even a first experimentation can be enough to start the tragic sequence that ends up with addiction.

However, this should not be interpreted to mean that only people with emotional problems can become addicted. The action of the habit-forming drug is such that it produces physical effects on anyone who uses it, and as the studies have shown over the years, *a physical craving for a narcotic will be built up in anyone who uses it continually, regardless of whether he is "normal" or disturbed.* Furthermore, the physical addiction will start to build with frightening speed.

Therefore, all experimentation must be regarded as risky. And this applies even to drugs that are not known to be physically addictive, like amphetamine and marihuana. For a youngster who is fooling around with them is very likely in the frame of mind to try drugs that will give him a stronger "kick," to say nothing of the emotional dependence that might build up.

The sooner you act if you suspect that your youngster is exposed to drug abuse or actually involved, the better are the chances of preventing the tragedy of addiction. Experts describe a process of addiction that has three more or less distinct stages:

Stage one is the period of initiation to the drug.

In stage two the habit is being built up and the body and mind become dependent. The victim wants more, and feels that he needs it. Certainly, this is far more dangerous than the first stage, for it usually means that the young person is well on his way to full dependence. Yet not everyone who reaches stage two goes all the way. There is still a chance of heading off the worst.

The third stage is that of full addiction. In a literal sense, the victim is enslaved by the drug.

Clearly you have to take action as soon as your suspicions are aroused. Delay increases the danger. But it is just as important that you do not panic, not become hysterical, not be rash. You must inform yourself of the proper steps to take—and then take them, promptly but *calmly*.

The discussions in this book will serve as a guide for what you should—and should not—do to prevent drug abuse by your child and to deal with it if it does occur.

3: How to Spot
the Use of Drugs

There are no simple, sure-fire rules for telling when a youngster has been using drugs. Even the physician has a problem, because the symptoms are seldom that definite, and the drug abuser is usually adept at convincing the doctor that something else is responsible for them. Similarly, the police, among the most experienced observers, will often be hard put to prove their suspicions. As a parent, however, you have an advantage. You will be aware of significant changes in behavior or physical appearance that a stranger or casual acquaintance might not detect.

Following are some of the symptoms that may indicate drug use, as gathered from medical and police sources.[1] It is impossible to list them with great precision or in exact order. Individuals differ in their physical and emotional responses, and effects vary somewhat according to the amount and frequency of drug abuse, the kind of drug, and whether it is used alone or in combination with others.

- *Abrupt changes in behavior, such as—*
- *—loss of interest in sports and other activities;*

[1] See especially: *Narcotics and Narcotics Addiction,* 2nd edition, Charles C. Thomas Publisher, 1962.

—*staying out of school;*
—*a dropping level of attention to school work.*

• *Disinterest in the opposite sex.*

• *Moodiness.*

• *A tendency to sit looking off into the distance, called by addicts "goofing"; this may be due to the use of either heroin or barbiturates or both.*

• *Sudden carelessness in appearance, particularly if the youngster has been neat in the past; this may indicate onsetting barbiturate dependency.*

• *Drowsiness and lethargy; if this is accompanied by excessive itching, it could mean an overdose of one of the opiates.*

• *A tendency to laugh excessively or to laugh at things no one else thinks are funny, or he says or does strange things that suggest his mind is distorting time and space; he may be mildly high on marihuana.*

• *An appearance of intoxication, but there is no smell of alcohol; he could be taking marihuana or barbiturates or sniffing glue. The conditions differ somewhat. Marihuana tends to produce the hilarious type of intoxication. Barbiturates tend to bring about stupor when used in sufficient amounts. The word "tend" is important, for the differences are not always clear-cut, and there are degrees of intoxication. If a person has just smoked marihuana, he will have a distinctive "weedy" odor on his breath.*

• *A "hopped-up" appearance—bright, shiny eyes, when usually his look is that of a fairly calm person; this may be the result of using barbiturates or amphetamine, or possibly marihuana.*

• *Mixing with new companions who seem to be given to drinking and smoking and seeking their night-time pleasures in disreputable places or where marihuana is reported to be widely used; he stays out much later than usual and gives evasive answers when questioned about his whereabouts.*

• *The use of words that have an odd, underworld tinge, which could indicate that he has been consorting with questionable persons.*

• *Frequent conversation about drugs with his friends and the avid reading of books and articles on the subject.*

• *Loss of appetite, perhaps with a rapid loss of weight; this often happens when the use of sleeping or pep pills begins.*

• *Or just the reverse—a sudden great increase in appetite accompanied by wild raids on the refrigerator, which is a common aftereffect of marihuana smoking.*

• *Fluctuations in the wideness of the pupils of*

the eyes not accounted for by changes in light intensity; immediately after an injection of heroin or the use of some other opiates the pupils contract.

• *Undue seclusiveness, such as the youngster's locking himself in the bathroom or bedroom for hours at a time.*

• *Desperation for money, when you can't see what he needs it for; this could mean that he has already developed a habit.*

• *Mysterious disappearance of pawnable or sale-able items belonging to the youngster or other members of the household; addicts are often driven to thievery to get money to buy drugs. Of course, if he steals from friends or strangers, ad-diction should immediately be suspected as the cause.*

It is important to keep in mind that none of these peculiarities of behavior or physical appearance is necessarily caused by the use of drugs. Drowsiness, apparent intoxication, glazed eyes, the loss of appe-tite, and so on are symptoms of many diseases. Most normal adolescents at one time or another become moody, change their interests abruptly, lose interest in the opposite sex for periods, and even skip school. When a youngster's behavior is extremely different from what it is usualiy, or if he steals, a psychological upset could be the cause. There is no way you can tell for sure. But under the circumstances, with the use of drugs as widespread as it is, you must be suspicious and probe further. There are certain things you might look for.

• *Pills of any sort or cough medicine which have not been prescribed specifically for your youngster by a doctor.*

• *Airplane glue, paints, lacquers, thinners, cleaning fluids, gasoline, ether, lighter fluid, nail polish, or any similar substance giving off fumes that create dizziness or numbness.*

• *Cigarette papers or a pipe (especially one with a small bowl); these are used for smoking marihuana. The drug itself most often is in the form of black or dark brown powder or flakes. Sometimes, in its less pure—and cheaper—forms, tiny pieces of twig and other earthy matter are mixed in it.*

• *A white, crystalline or flaky powder looking like epsom salts, with a bitter taste but no odor; this would be cocaine, a stimulant, which is either sniffed or injected.*

• *Heroin, a fine white powder that looks like milk sugar; sometimes it is dull grey or reddish-brown.*

• *A hypodermic syringe and needle; the former might be homemade from an eyedropper. This equipment is used, of course, for injecting heroin or cocaine.*

• *A cooking spoon, in which heroin is melted to*

the right consistency for injection; this is usually an ordinary kitchen spoon whose handle has been bent back, although sometimes a small bottle cap with a wire handle or a small glass vial will be used. The bottoms of these "cookers" are often blackened by the match flames used to melt the drug.

And on his body you might find:

● *Black and blue spots resembling tattoo marks on the youngster's arms and legs or on the backs of his hands; this comes from "skin-popping"— that is, injecting the drug under the skin; small scabs or crusts over the spots indicate recent injections.*

● *Long scars, frequently looking like tattoos, along the veins, especially those of the forearms, backs of the hands, insteps, and lower abdomen; the scars, or "tracks," are caused by the collapse of the veins due to continual injection of the narcotic into them.*

Of course, if you don't find any drugs or equipment and don't see any scars, you should not conclude that your suspicions were unfounded. Drug users are skillful in hiding evidence and disguising the symptoms. (Usually, it takes a long while for parents to discover what is happening—two or more years is common.) Furthermore, except in the case of the barbiturate user, who tends to become sloppy, there isn't much difference in appearance between an addict and other people. The writer sat one morning in a big-city courtroom alongside the judge, observing the arraignments of narcotics-law violators. At least a dozen young male and female addicts were brought before us at the bench, including one young man who had just come out of a state of unconsciousness and stood there blinking at us in his undershirt and trousers. Not one looked like the emaciated, sore-ridden dope fiend of legend. Instead, all looked like perfectly normal people, some neat, some not, and in varying degrees of bodily huskiness. Probably the best dressed person in the courtroom was a twenty-one-year-old suburban addict arrested for possession of heroin. The state of dress and general appearance tended to reflect economic level and style of living rather than the use of drugs.

Ultimately, it may require a laboratory test plus corroborative evidence to prove legally whether or not a person is taking narcotics. Two tests are in use, the Nalline and the urine. The Nalline test is employed in the California rehabilitation program for control of probationers. A chemical is injected into the person suspected of taking heroin or any other opiate, and if he is, a very quick reaction will be quickly produced. The test has been criticized as undignified and cruel, and its use is apparently declining. California authorities claim it has helped them to achieve a 30 percent abstention rate. Urine analysis is less controversial and considered more reliable and flexible by its proponents on the ground that it will detect the presence of any drug. This test is not as yet generally available to many private physicians.

It is easy to see why, as a layman, you cannot rely on your own diagnosis. Even the medical professionals do not have an easy time of it, although the current stepped-up pace of education within the field is undoubtedly improving the general knowledge of physicians. If, therefore, you suspect your youngster is taking drugs, don't make accusations, don't condemn, get him to a physician right away. If this doesn't work in your area, if, for example, your physician feels ill-equipped to handle the case, or just does not want to, look for other professional assistance, as suggested in other parts of this volume.

4: What to Do If
You Learn that Your
Youngster Is Sniffing Glue
or Taking Cough Medicine

Glue-sniffing is the way many youngsters start on drugs. They are too young to have money of their own in sufficient amounts to buy ordinary narcotics or to associate with the marihuana and pill users, who won't have anything to do with "kids." They will use whatever they can lay their hands on, once they get going: airplane glue, paints, lacquers, thinners, cleaning fluids, gasoline, lighter fluids, ether. (Gasoline and cleaning fluids, such as carbon tetrachloride, can be deadly indeed, worse than glue.) Plastic cements and airplane glues are easily purchased in tube form from hobby shops, candy stores, and supermarkets. The price, about fifteen cents a tube, is low enough for the third-grader—yes, we are speaking about children at even that tender age.

While sniffing can start rather innocently—the child may build a model airplane or submarine and just find himself liking the smell of the glue—the real danger usually arises when a youngster in a group finds out that you can get "dizzy" or "feel funny" if you inhale the vapor long enough. He then becomes the source of supply for the others, who may or may not continue to sniff.

When the youngster sniffs glue, he becomes intoxicated. At first he experiences a pleasant, hazy, light feeling. Often, this is followed by distortion of the senses. He may suddenly find himself with double vision, ringing in the ears, and hallucinations. His speech slurs, and he is unsteady, unable to control his bodily movements. A half hour to forty-five minutes later, he becomes drowsy. A stupor sets in, and in many instances he cannot recall what happened earlier. This stage lasts about an hour. In general, the glue sniffer acts like someone who is drunk on alcohol, but the effect is potentially much more dangerous.

An overdose of gasoline or carbon tetrachloride can destroy large areas of brain tissue. The central nervous system, liver, and kidneys can be damaged. As a result of glue-sniffing, aggressive impulses that are ordinarily kept under control can be released. You may have read in the newspaper about a case in which a boy stabbed and seriously wounded a man when under the influence of the drug, then was barely able to remember what he did. Sometimes, the youngster will suffer from delusions of grandeur, as in the case of a boy who attacked four marines, or another who, believing he could fly like superman, jumped from a roof and suffered severe injuries. The drug may bring to the surface a self-destructive tendency which can be terribly dangerous, as in the case of the boy who placed himself on a railroad track and was barely saved from the wheels of an approaching train. Most of the time, however, the glue-sniffer will withdraw into his own fantasy life, as other drug users do.

Of course, inhaling paints, lacquers, thinners, ether, and similar substances can have the same bad effects as glue-sniffing.

This is ordinarily the easiest type of drug abuse to stop, because the boy or girl is still probably young enough to be controlled successfully by adults, and because for most of those who try sniffing it is a passing fad, just another childish adventure. Your main concern should be with the youngster's health, not with whether he is misbehaving. You want him to stop playing with the dangerous materials in order to prevent him from hurting himself. Your attitude should be the same as when you found him playing with matches in his infant years.

First, there are some *don'ts* and these apply under all circumstances, whether the youngster is sniffing glue, smoking marihuana, or taking drugs in any other forms.

- *Don't panic, or become hysterical.*

- *Don't immediately accuse the child of being bad.*

- *Don't strike him.*

- *Don't call the police.*

- *Don't rush him to the hospital.*

- *Don't have him committed anywhere.*

- *If a school teacher or administrator calls you up and tells you that you ought to be aware of suspicious symptoms or behavior, don't react, as*

*some parents do, with anger or with the charge
that your boy is being unfairly accused and that
the nasty insinuations can't possibly be true. The
school people are to be congratulated for being
aware of the problem and wanting to help.*

Having found out that your child is sniffing glue or
some other such substance, your primary concern is
to determine if any physical damage has been done.
Have him checked by a physician immediately. It is
unwise to rely on his testimony as to the amount of
inhaling he has done, for he can be inaccurate without realizing it. If he has been at it for any length of
time or has breathed large amounts of vapor, it may
be necessary to hospitalize him for observation and
treatment. Your physician will determine whether
that is called for. Most of the time, it will not be.

This is the time the youngster can be talked to
most effectively, since the physical examination will
dramatize the potential danger of sniffing. His mis-
behavior in all likelihood stems from adventurousness, and it is fairly easy to convince him now that
what he has been doing is a terrible mistake and
should stop. The chances are he will.

Who should do the talking? If you have a good
relationship with him, if he is accustomed to being
guided by you, if he "listens" when you admonish
him, then by all means sit down with him and set him
straight. But if there is any problem of communication between you, the person who does the serious
talking should be some outsider who can provide the
authority without bringing into play any of the
tensions that normally exist in the parent-child relationship.

This might be a physician, a school psychologist, a

teacher, a social worker, a minister, or even some acquaintance or relative of yours liked and respected by the youngster. In most cases a talk, along with a plain, old-fashioned, straight-from-the-shoulder laying down of the law, will bring an end to the dangerous experimenting. Sometimes, it will not be sufficient. If a physician or some other competent professional recommends consultation with a psychiatrist or psychologist, it is important that you comply, that you not be deterred from sensible action by foolish notions of shame or embarrassment. For what the professional suspects is that the glue-sniffing is fulfilling some emotional need, and he is suggesting you see someone better qualified than he to find out what it is and how to deal with it.

The emotional needs will, of course, differ from child to child. He may feel left out of things; the glue-sniffing is helping him "belong" to some group he wants to be part of. He may feel inadequate in some way; the glue is helping him escape from these feelings. It may be that there is a very serious emotional problem and that the sniffing is merely a symptom of it.

Much of the time, all that is required is a mild form of therapy, which in reality amounts to several talk-sessions with a qualified professional. He will help the youngster to understand why he is sniffing glue and assist him in directing his energies into more constructive ways.

Often, the counselor will be the physician who has been given the diagnosis and the recommendations for handling by a psychiatric colleague. Or it may be a school psychologist or a social worker.

The procedure is the same if you discover that your child is drinking cough medicine. Like glue and other intoxicating inhalants, cough medicine is relatively easy to obtain and inexpensive, and the effect is weak when compared to marihuana, barbiturates and heroin. Therefore, it is a drug of the younger set, in the early teens or below. But unlike glue, cough medicine may contain derivatives of opium, such as codeine, hycodan, dicodid, or percodan. The amount of codeine in an average bottle is actually small, and the "kicks" are derived as much from the alcohol contained in most cough medicines as from the drug. Nevertheless, the effects can be serious. It is imperative that you put a stop to the dangerous practice without delay.

As with the problem of glue-sniffing, these are the steps you should take:

1. Take the youngster to the doctor immediately for a thorough examination; if further examination or any treatment is necessary, have it done without delay, even if it requires hospitalization.

2. Talk with the youngster, explaining calmly and clearly the dangers of drinking cough medicine; if for any reason you feel you can't do it properly or if the child seems not to accept what you say, have a professional or a mature friend or relative talk with him.

3. If the need for psychiatric or other professional help is indicated, make arrangements promptly.

5: What to Do If Your Youngster Is Exposed to Drugs

You have some reason to think your child may be tempted to smoke marihuana or take pills, perhaps even to try heroin. There has been talk in the area, the papers have carried stories, you have overheard some students talking about drug use at the school your youngster attends. The circle of friends he is running around with is a bit too adventurous, and you can't be sure.

There are some who argue that it is best not to raise the issue and set off the child's curiosity, which might lead him to try the very thing you're afraid of. Anyway, this reasoning continues, probably nothing very much will happen, since the incidence of addiction, as everyone knows, is in reality small.

This approach is dangerous. If other youngsters are fooling around with drugs, yours will undoubtedly be curious, and unless he is properly steeled with knowledge about the perils, he may easily succumb to temptation. Once he begins, he has taken the first step that may lead to addiction. There is no way of your knowing in advance whether he is one of those with a predisposition toward drug usage. You cannot take the chance.

Moreover, it is a mistake to think you can just let things go because you believe he is informed on the subject or sufficiently armored intellectually to resist temptation under all conditions. This might be true, but it would be very unwise to take it for granted. You have to be absolutely sure that he is well informed, and a good intellect and strong moral center are guarantees only if they are sustained by accurate knowledge.

Therefore, the right thing to do is to have a talk with him.

You are probably already conjuring up a picture of your youngster sitting there in front of you, annoyed, combative, impatient, certain that you know nothing about the "really important things." It doesn't matter. Difficult and uncomfortable as you may think it's going to be, the effort has to be made.

Perhaps you are wondering how you can now assert yourself as a parent when you have been rather easygoing up to now. It may be that you haven't spoken seriously with him these past few years about the problems he is running into as he is growing up. That is all the more reason for you to talk with him now. If you are going to deal with the drug problem, you have to *function fully as a parent*. He may not understand what's at stake. You do and are responsible to him. Therefore, you have no choice but to act, as rationally and carefully, but as forcefully, as you can.

Very well, now you have him there before you. What do you say? The words must be your own, naturally, but there are certain things to be covered:

1. This is to be a discussion, not a lecture. You wish to learn as well as inform. Your manner should be calm, even if he becomes irritable.

2. You have heard about the use of drugs in the neighborhood or school. As a parent, you are naturally interested. You have full confidence in him, but the condition exists, and you want him to know you are concerned.

3. Even though it may be hard for him to imagine, you do understand some of the things that concern him. You understand, for example, that a young person likes to be part of the group, and how difficult it is to say "no" when "everyone else" is doing it.

4. You would like him to know how you feel and what you think about all this, even though he may not think you know much about what's "in" these modern days. Let him hear you out, anyway, even if he thinks he knows everything you are going to say. He has nothing to lose, and it will make you feel better. This semijocular approach may help get his attention long enough to agree to a serious talk.

5. You are not concerned with questions of morality, of right or wrong, only with his health and safety, and his future. This is natural for a parent, indeed it is your obligation, even if he sometimes wishes you wouldn't be so conscientious about it in stopping him from doing what he wants to.

6. *You regard the experimenting that's being talked about as serious and potentially dangerous. Has he been at any gatherings lately where it has been going on? You are concerned not only for him, although he is, of course, your primary concern, but for the safety and health of all youngsters in the area. If he says no, you might ask whether it is because he understands why you disapprove. You may learn that he is well informed about the dangers. In which case, you can tell him that you are now confident he will not be so foolish as to experiment should the opportunity arise.*

7. *If it is apparent that he has no real information, or that he is misinformed—which can be more dangerous—you might very briefly run down the reasons why experimenting is unwise.*

8. *If he indicated that he has already been tempted, that one or more of his companions, for example, have tried marihuana or pills at a party or get-together, you might then ask—as calmly and casually as you can—whether he has tried the stuff himself.*

a) If the answer is no, *you might ask why. What were the reasons the others gave for trying, and what were his for not? The important thing here is to get as clear a picture as you can at this point of the thinking of the group your boy is part of.*

b) If the answer is yes, *again ask why. Did it seem like fun? Was it in response to a dare? Did he know what it really was that he was trying? It is important to determine how serious this is*

*to him, that is, whether he looks upon it as
simply one more, rather meaningless, adventure
or as something he is obviously intending to
indulge in again, perhaps with some regularity.
You might ask him whether he can tell you why
he thinks the fellows who first brought the drug
around did so. Was it to make an impression, to
appear important? Does he need that kind of
crutch?*

*9. If he has experimented, then now is the time
to make it clear you disapprove, not for reasons
of conventional morality, but because you know
it is dangerous. If he has tried marihuana you
may run into the "non-addicting" argument, and
you should be prepared with the material in
Chapter Six.*

If you have a fundamentally sound relationship
with the youngster and you are not unaccustomed to
putting your foot down firmly and getting results—in
short, if your instinct is to move with the forcefulness
and authority of an old-fashioned parent in a time of
need—then by all means, do so. But you must re-
strain any impulse to lash out with bitter, denuncia-
tory words and must demonstrate the genuineness of
your concern with his safety rather than with "saving
your own face."

In fact, whether you are used to acting authorita-
tively or not, you might have to, especially if the
youngster is going around with a group who are
definitely known to be drug users.

In America today, the teenager is more apt to run
with his pals than his parents. Sociologists refer to
your child's friends as his "peer-group" and warn

that its magnetic pull must not be underestimated. If his peer-group as a whole uses drugs, the likelihood is that sooner or later your youngster will, too. The more deeply he becomes involved with the narcotics "subculture"—that is the users, their ideas, their outlook on life, the whole narcotics atmosphere—the more certain it is he will go all the way and the harder it will be to prevent addiction if he starts taking drugs.

Some specialists in the field insist that when a boy or girl is associating with narcotics users no compromise is possible, and swift, surgical-like treatment is necessary. Dr. Daniel Casriel, medical supervisor of Daytop Village holds this view. "The family has to take a very decisive, definitive, positive, physical approach." He told the author: *"They have to rip that kid away from the group with which he's been associating.* If he is running around with a group of a half dozen or so kids who are doing this, he has to be prevented from seeing them! This can be done by telling him he can't do it. He can't be with those friends. He must be encouraged to develop new friends and patterns of behavior and activity which are away from this.

"The parent can say something like: 'You're getting into trouble whether you can see it or not. As long as you're a dependent of mine and I'm your boss, there are certain things that I'm not going to let you do. I don't want you to be with those people because they take drugs. *You're going to have to cut them out and start with new friends.* I don't care what you think about it. You're not going to do it! You're going to have to develop new friends and a new way of life that doesn't involve you in this!' "

The youngster may insist that even though his

friends are taking the drugs, he won't. Dr. Casriel answers:

"When you're in a steam room, you get sweaty. When you're with people who take pills, you're going to take them sooner or later. If you don't you're going to feel like an outsider. Why do you have to put yourself in that position? The second you get on the wrong train to Philadelphia, you're only a foot away from where you should be. If you continue on that wrong train, you'll never get off it. You can't see where that train is leading them, but I can, because of my age, experience, maturity, and perspective. You have to choose between me and your friends. When you're twenty-one, you can do what you want, but now you can't. Until then, you're my ward and I want to give you the best help that I know how. Also, taking drugs is illegal. You can meet other friends who don't do it."

Note that Dr. Casriel will go so far as to say that the parent should make it clear that in this situation, whether the child agrees or not, or likes it or not, it just has to be the way the parent wants it. This may seem arbitrary and insensitive, but in Dr. Casriel's view it is the only sane course, because of the great pulling power of a teenager's friendships.

"Such a strong position is necessary because the youngster may not be strong enough to make his own decision. Now, if he has a very strong personal attachment to his friends, it's even more reason to give them up. Remember, you are not preventing the child from doing other things that other adolescents do— date, socialize, and so forth. If you're tolerant in other areas where you can afford to be tolerant, the kid knows that you're not rigid. And if you're a successful citizen, respected by yourself, your wife, your community, he is going to respect your opinion—so long as you're not a tyrant.

"I would treat this on a very personal basis. I would say: 'Look, son, if I saw you taking poison, I would knock it out of your hand. Or if I saw a car coming at you, I would push you out of the way, even if I had to break your leg in doing it. This is what I see with the drugs.' "

Having laid down the law, what do you do to enforce it if the youngster refuses to obey? To begin with, Dr. Casriel urges, as do most other authorities, that professional assistance be enlisted, because prevention and treatment tend to merge, the goal being to change the young person's way of living. However, he cautions you against thinking that thereby you get rid of your responsibility. While the professional might administer therapy, if it is necessary, or counsel the youngster, you must do everything you can to prevent him from going out with his drug-using friends. You must try to occupy his free time. He should not be permitted to have excess money—that is, more than he needs for carfare to school, lunches, and other day-to-day necessaries. You must try to keep close tabs on where and with whom he is at all times. That is more or less the negative aspect of what you ought to do. There is a more positive aspect, which Dr. Casriel points out:

"The parents should encourage him to open up new avenues of interest, to seek out other forms of entertainment, relaxation, pleasure. If necessary, they should take the child out of his delinquent group or school and send him to a different school—if they have the money, perhaps to a private school. If he lives in the city, they should take him away from his summer haunts if they can, send him to camp. If funds allow, even a well-guarded travel vacation is useful—get him where he can learn other things about life besides where to get drugs, where the pusher is, and the like. In other words, he should be distracted as much as possible in a constructive manner, away from the pursuit of a way of life which can become fatal."

6: What to Do If
Your Youngster Is
Smoking Marihuana

The scene: a high school auditorium. The students have just seen a film on the evils of drug addiction. A doctor rises, goes to the podium and stands ready to answer questions.

A student asks, "Doctor, is marihuana addicting?" The doctor replies, "No but. . . ."

No one hears the rest of what he says. The students look at one another and grin. They have heard what they wanted to hear. They wink at each other. They feel perfectly safe now in smoking marihuana, for didn't the doctor say it wasn't addicting?

As one student later reported: "The film was a complete failure. Once that doctor talked the way he did, he gave the kids the exact excuse they needed to continue to use 'pot' [as marihuana is colloquially called]. From the moment he said the word 'no,' they paid no attention whatever to anything else he said."

This incident, which actually happened in an Eastern suburban school, illustrates the difficulty you run into when you try to discourage youngsters from smoking marihuana. They think that they have investigated the matter and are quite convinced it is safe.

Their main argument is that marihuana is non-addicting and therefore not to be considered dangerous in the way heroin is. They maintain also, that the laws against marihuana make no sense. If there's nothing wrong with using alcohol for kicks, why should there be anything wrong in using "pot"? All it does is make you "high." It's silly to claim that smoking marihuana leads to the use of heroin, they say, because they can point to many people who have smoked it and have not gone on to heroin, or for that matter, have not had anything bad happen to them.

The younger teenager looks toward his college elder for justification, finding in campus use of marihuana corroboration of his view that it is the "in" thing to use today. Richard Goldstein, in his book *1 in 7,* writes about the prevalence of marihuana smoking in the colleges:

"Administrators deny it, and alumni doubt it. But the police know about it. Health officials and school psychiatrists are aware of it. The students themselves are not only sure [marihuana smoking] exists, they can usually tell you where to find [the marihuana]. In Harvard Square you can obtain marihuana within thirty minutes. Near Columbia University, on upper Broadway, it takes twenty minutes. And in Sausalito, with the aid of willing Berkeley students, the source is only a short car-ride from Sproul Hall. . . . Marihuana has become this generation's alcohol. . . . The pot party is anywhere. It occurs beneath white porticoes of fraternity houses, or inside tents especially constructed on handy rooftops so that party goers can observe nature when they get high. Usually it's at a student's apartment, away from prying parental eyes."

The college behavior is being imitated on the high school level. Figures are impossible to find, but most observers agree that there has been a marked increase in marihuana usage among the younger set, particularly seniors in the large metropolitan-area high schools.

Sooner or later, your youngster will very likely be exposed to marihuana and may try it himself. You might detect the symptoms—the drunken laughter, the staggering, the glazed eyes, the inability to judge time and space accurately, the compulsive eating. You might come across the cigarette paper, the pipe, or the drug itself. Or it simply might be that some reliable person such as a school administrator or parent informs you that your youngster is smoking marihuana.

Just how concerned should you really be? Is marihuana so bad? Is it any worse, for example, than alcohol?

You should indeed be concerned—but not terrified. The dangers are quite real, although not as great as you might fear. The Medical Society of the County of New York, in a policy statement, "The Dangerous Drug Problem," describes marihuana as a "mild hallucinogen;" it produces hallucinations and intoxication without being physically habit forming. In that respect, "pot" is no worse than alcohol. But the similarity really stops there, especially because it takes very little marihuana to produce the sort of "high" that ordinarily results only from drinking large quantities of alcohol. By the time a drunk decides to do something he shouldn't, he may very well be too tipsy to be able to carry it out. The marihuana smoker doesn't lose muscular control for a long time, not until he's taken a lot of the drug; he is thus much more liable to do foolish and dangerous things than a drunk is. This is in addition to certain other dangers not commonly associated with drinking.

In 1944, Mayor Fiorello La Guardia, of New York, concerned over the near-panic that had been aroused in the city in the late 'thirties and early 'forties over an alleged marihuana epidemic in the high schools, asked the New York Academy of Medicine to undertake a thorough study. The report, possibly the most comprehensive yet published on the subject, shows that while marihuana is indeed for the most part a mild hallucinogenic, marihuana smoking frequently produces physical and psychological effects which can cause serious trouble:

1. It loosens inner restraints or inhibitions. *The user is highly suggestible. Girls are more liable to be seduced while under the influence of the drug. Youngsters can be led to do things for a lark which are either dangerous or criminal, and wind up in jail.*

2. It can bring emotional conflicts to the surface. *If a person has a tendency toward psychosis, marihuana could push him over the edge. There are many cases on record where marihuana smoking has preceded attempts at suicide, and innumerable instances in the police files all over the country where such usage has directly preceded the commission of murder. No one is arguing that marihuana causes people to murder, only that it can easily act as a "trigger" to release murderous impulses. Moreover, it can lead to feelings of dread and anxiety, following a brief "high." The Mayor's Committee conducted*

*experiments on the effects of marihuana smoking
and reported that "in three of the subjects a
definite psychotic state occurred, in two, shortly
after the marihuana ingestion, in one after a
two-week interval."*

3. It affects the ability to respond correctly to
danger. *The Mayor's Committee found that
marihuana temporarily causes the mind to function poorly, depending on how much is smoked;
the body and hands lose their steadiness, the
sense of time is altered—things seem to last
longer. This is especially dangerous when driv-
ing a car.*

One of the most terrifying youthful pranks is going
for a "pot" spin. A group of young people will drive
slowly along the highway enjoying a marihuana high.
To them it seems romantic, but they are incapable of
sizing up the danger or dealing properly with emer-
gencies.

Why such things happen has only recently become
clear with the isolation of the ingredient in marihuana which is responsible. It is known as *tetrahydro-
cannabinol,* abbreviated as THC. Describing his experimental use of THC on a patient to a national
conference on psychedelic drugs held in Chicago in
the Spring of 1968, Dr. Donald R. Jasinski, of the
National Institute of Mental Health, reported the
subject had developed visual hallucinations, distortions of sensory perceptions, loss of insight, muscle
rigidity and muteness. "He later related that he felt
detached from his body, saw himself shrivel down to
a doll and witnessed his own funeral." As reported in
the press, Dr. Joseph H. Skom, chairman of the

Illinois State Medical Society, said the report drives home the potential peril in marihuana use. "If users get enough THC in the stuff they are buying, they are facing a hazard," he says. Similarly, Dr. Harris Isbell of the federal addiction research center in Lexington, Ky., commented that the THC experiment clearly indicated the importance of the size of the dosage. The fact, then, that most users do not experience psychotic episodes means only that the reefers are relatively low in THC content. The point is becoming clearer all the time: we are dealing with potential hazards, and it is foolish for a normal person to become involved with marihuana.

4. It is often the first step to the use of heroin. *While not every marihuana user goes on to heroin, the majority of heroin users have started with marihuana. It's easy to go from one drug to another.*

"In the last decade," drug authority Charles Winick writes in a study called *Marihuana Use By Young People,* "much of the renewed interest in marihuana has stemmed from its being a precursor of the use of the addicting opiates, among teenagers and young adults.

"There are many reasons young people who start with marihuana 'graduate' to the opiates. They may try heroin on a dare, of a sort common among teenagers, and find they enjoy it. Young people may originally try marihuana because it is forbidden and the object of so many taboos. They may drift into the use of opiates, which are even more taboo. The 'kick' of marihuana may become less stimulating, and the young sensation seeker may decide to try the stronger 'kick' of heroin."

Many youngsters take marihuana, because they are having personality difficulties, and the smoking makes them feel better about themselves. But since the drug does not really help them solve their problems, "they may then go on to the use of opiates in an unconscious effort to solve the same problems. . . . Some marihuana users take the drug before going to social situations with which they feel inadequate, especially situations including girls."

Moreover, because marihuana has been illegal for so long the Federal narcotics law lumps marihuana together with heroin and other true narcotics—its use has become deeply intertwined with the underworld pattern of life. It has attracted the same kind of people who are attracted to narcotics—the troubled, the disturbed, the lonely, the outcast, the criminal. And the patterns of distribution are similar. Thus, where you find marihuana, the chances are that sooner or later you will run into heroin. One contact leads to another, one social setting to another, one pusher to another.

5. It does create psychological and emotional dependence. *This is the reason the World Health Organization regards marihuana as a dangerous drug. Even though physiological addiction doesn't take place as it does with heroin or the barbiturates, continued usage creates real psychological dependence; the user learns he can escape from his problems and the world through it. In other words, since the habitual user is already likely to be a disturbed individual, marihuana easily becomes an emotional crutch.*

6. It may lead to withdrawal from the world. *In the final analysis, this may be the most insidious effect of all. The youngster learns to "tune out" reality when things are uncomfortable. He ceases to function as he should, for he begins to prefer to live in a dream world.*

It is clear, therefore, that you must be very concerned about marihuana smoking. However, in itself the drug is much less harmful than any of the others, and damaging effects on the body are the exception rather than the rule. There is no need to rush the youngster to the doctor. Your first step—and this might well be the only one you have to take—is to explain to him the dangers of the drug. (If you think it better, have someone else, preferably a professional, talk with him.) The following discussion of marihuana by Dr. Henry Brill, Vice-Chairman of the New York State Narcotic Control Commission and Director of Pilgrim State Hospital, could serve as a basis for what you say.

"Marihuana has been known almost since the beginning of time, almost as long as alcohol. It has never achieved permanent social acceptance anywhere, and those countries that have had the longest experience with it finally have been forced to try to get rid of it and to make its use illegal because of its severe social effects." Referring to users in the Far East and Middle East, Dr. Brill says, "These people are turned inward, live from one moment to another. Their constructive capacity is reduced to zero. They just survive. Now translate that into our own situation. If taken to the point of intoxication, marihuana is more dangerous than alcohol, because it produces hallucinations and distortions of space and time. The effect of continuing use on the mental life of the individual has to be a withdrawing from activity toward inactivity. And then, of course, once you have an involvement with a life which chiefly looks inward and not outward to practical accomplishment, you open the door to other drug experiences.

"I think the philosophy that goes along with it is a particularly vicious one. It is that one lives for the internal experience, that internal reality takes precedence over external reality, and that physical comfort and pleasure are to be chosen over the discomforts of doing something constructive. Among the constructive things that people do is to get trained. And this hits at a point when the effort and stress for training for a future life are very great on young people. It offers them a beautiful chance to retreat. It erodes away the necessary capacity for the work that all of us face.

"Marihuana has this tendency. People will tell you that this isn't true, that what it does, is to release the tensions, make one more comfortable for the time being, so that you are able to return to work more effectively. But it doesn't work out that way. The effect is too strong. It does more than merely relax the tension. It distorts perception and produces all sorts of subjective experiences which already are far beyond that level. It is a *hallucinogen,* not as strong as LSD, but it belongs in the same general category."

As to the argument that marihuana is not an addictive drug, Dr. Brill points out: "The importance of the relationship between the drug and the man is that *if the man is enslaved in the drug experience, he is habituated.* The physical symptoms are the least important of all drug manifestations, the easiest to overcome. The problem is of *living for the drug experience,* and the individual who lives for the drug experience, no matter which drug, is in trouble. The tendency to live for the drug experience occurs quite frequently with marihuana."

In addition you ought to stress the fact that possession of marihuana is a Federal offense—and a serious offense. The law applies to users as well as sellers, and the penalties are heavy:

For a first offense of possession: imprisonment of from two to ten years, with probation and parole permitted.

For a second possession or first selling offense: a mandatory sentence of from five to twenty years with parole and probation excluded.

For a third possession or second and subsequent selling offense: mandatory ten to forty years' imprisonment with parole and probation excluded.

An arrest and court record can have serious consequences. For example, the boy could be denied entrance to law school as a result. Moreover, the recent upsurge of drug abuse may very well lead to even harsher legal penalties rather than lighter. From the very practical, immediate human point of view, the question of whether marihuana should be legalized or the law made less severe is irrelevant. These are matters of *social action,* not to be confused with the question of whether the individual should risk his entire future by breaking the law now.

It would probably do a lot of good if, after explaining the dangers, you laid down your own law. Whether the youngster accepts what you have explained about marihuana or not, he is forbidden to use it again. A New York editor told the author what happened in the case of his own son: "We became convinced that our sixteen-year-old was smoking marihuana, with his friends. We smelled it in his room. I'd smelled it often before, having been brought up around Greenwich Village. There were also other indications. He became chronically peevish, sometimes he would seem a little drunk, and his eyes looked strange, rather glassy. The windows were open when they should not have been. He and his friends discussed narcotics a lot; they had a great deal of interest in the subject, an inordinate interest. My boy is a prolific reader, and you can tell what he's interested in by what he's reading. He'd taken out every single book on narcotics he could find. Once we came home unexpectedly and found there had been marihuana smoked.

"When we found out, we talked with him. He was argumentative, and refused to accept the facts about the danger of the drug. Finally we simply forbade him to smoke it again. If he did, we warned him, he would be deprived of his allowance, would have to take his lunches to school instead of being given money to buy them, and other punishments would be imposed. He knew that these weren't empty threats, because we had never had compunctions about punishing him when we thought it necessary. As far as we know, he gave up smoking marihuana.

"But it actually was not the threat that worked so much as our authoritative attitude. Our experience with him and the experience of friends who have children of his age is that the child wants to be discovered and prevented, wants the parents to put their foot down, to be stern and act in an authoritative manner when it comes to something as serious as this —when he knows that something he gets into is wrong. When parents fail to keep their eyes open and to intervene, the child often feels insecure. He cannot depend upon them. He must be able to count on them to do for him what he cannot do for himself. Our boy feels parental discipline is part of love and will often do things he knows to be wrong in order to get us to make this act of love. Children want their parents to be authoritative. It's not a good relationship to be on equal terms."

If the youngster persists in using the drug, you will certainly have to seek professional help. You should consult your family physician, your minister, or perhaps the school psychologist, someone who in talking with the youngster can tell whether there seems to be an emotional problem which needs to be treated. The probability is, though, that his friends are smoking marihuana, and he hasn't stopped and still won't because if he does he will no longer be "in."

Unless you catch it early, marihuana usage is difficult to break because the young person has found in it a congenial way of life, which is providing him with considerable social satisfaction. To begin with, he learns how to smoke and enjoy it in the company of more experienced users. This gives him a feeling of being "in" with the group, especially attractive to a youngster because it's daring to indulge in a forbidden and dangerous pleasure. He may find that these get-togethers are fun, because the inhibitions vanish, and the conversation flows easily.

Under no circumstances must you throw up your hands in despair. Meet with the parents of the other youngsters and with the school authorities to discuss ways of keeping an eye on the youngsters. If there is a youth board in your community, appeal to them for help. Since youngsters rarely smoke marihuana when they are alone, concerted action by the parents, professionals, and authorities, could bring the "pot parties" to an end, thus removing a major cause of the problem. It might be a long and hard battle, but it is one you have to win.

7: What to Do If
You Fear Your Youngster
May Try LSD or
Other Hallucinogens

In recent years a relatively new and very powerful hallucinogenic drug generally known as LSD (the letters stand for lysergic acid diethylamide 25) has been the subject of an intense debate that, unfortunately, has tended to glamorize it. The result is that LSD has emerged as a symbol of revolt against conventional standards and morality. Those who are part of the LSD "movement" believe it can be used to free the human personality, to liberate the inner man from excessive concern with the externals of life. They say that use of the drug might enable a person to achieve an understanding of the world and union with the universe, perhaps even a mystical experience. Missionaries like Timothy Leary expound its virtues with religious zeal; indeed, he has founded a religious cult based upon use of LSD. Inevitably, LSD has attracted the drug-experimenting college student, and inevitably, as black-market production has increased, it has found its way down the age scale to the high school and even the grade school student.

Whether or not a greater understanding of the

world, or even a mystical experience, can result from taking LSD, is beside the point. We are concerned here with something else—the threat of LSD to the physical and mental well-being of your child. The facts concerning the proper usage and dangers of the drug are quite clear, and all but the most rabid adherents of the LSD cult accept them. There should be no difficulty in setting them before your boy or girl. Unless the youngster is too seriously disturbed for rational argument to make an impression, he should respond.

That LSD is potentially an exciting new psychiatric tool is perfectly true. It gives promise in the treatment of neurosis, schizophrenia, and alcoholism, and is being experimented with in "depth psychiatry." But scientists do not yet understand how it functions, nor can they predict when the results will be beneficial or even how long they will last.

In his book *The Beyond Within,* one of the country's foremost experts on the subject, Dr. Sydney Cohen of the University of California in Los Angeles, who has conducted research on LSD for over ten years, states that the drug "seems to trigger a depth charge into the unconscious processes." It releases mysterious chemical processes in the brain that proceed long after the drug has been eliminated. What happens after that depth charge explodes depends on the nature of the person, the way he feels that day, what he is surrounded with and whom he is with at the time he takes LSD.

Even when the treatment helps the patient to achieve the self-understanding he is after, the experience can be terribly agonizing and fearsome. Not everyone can endure "the guilt-ridden memories" that pour "over the floodgates drenching the sufferers with sweat and tears," says Dr. Cohen. "Not everyone is able to pass through to the other side of the anguish."

The great danger is the possibility of kicking off a psychotic state with LSD. One such case was that of a secretary who said she had taken the drug between two hundred and three hundred times in the preceding three years, along with other drugs. At first, she thought she was being helped—the drugs were "unblocking" her. Later, the experiences became frightening. She found herself unable to control her emotions. She became panicky, unable to think clearly, afraid of the recurring hallucinations, such as skulls of people she knew moving around the room. She had to take large doses of sedatives to quiet her during the day and allow her to sleep at night. What had happened was simply that she had been given too many drug treatments by the therapist, who was a believer in LSD.

A ten-year-old boy accidentally consumed a sugar cube containing LSD which his detective-father had confiscated from a pusher. The child had a severe reaction for several days, which gradually became less upsetting but did not completely subside. A week later, he was still nervous, especially when he saw movements on the TV screen while the set was off. When he tried to study, the words in his books would waver. He was treated with a combination of psychotherapy and tranquilizers. It took six weeks to make a full recovery.

The author of this book sat with two investigators of the New York State Narcotics Bureau in Albany. They told him of just having visited a near-by hospital to see an 18-year-old college girl who had thoughtlessly succumbed to the LSD temptation. It was her first experience. She had gone into a psychotic state, which required hospitalization. "She hasn't come out of it yet," said one of the investigators. "It's been a month!"

LSD is not considered addicting in the conventional sense. Often, patients who have benefited from one carefully administered dose in a medical setting will not want to take it again. Dr. Cohen, however, warns that the full story is not yet in, and that "habituation to the psychological effects of this group of drugs is possible, in certain personality types. Passive-dependent and psychopathic individuals with access to large supplies have used them uncounted times and have had difficulty in breaking themselves of the habit."

In 1967, the press began to report startling cases in which LSD symptoms were reappearing six months after the drug had been consumed! Perhaps the most unsettling of all the most recent reports are those which indicate LSD may have profound effects on the genes, which transmit our hereditary traits, and that if it is taken during pregnancy may result in unpredictably deformed infants.

It is the unpredictableness of LSD which is the greatest danger in use by the layman. No other drug is as dangerous as LSD when used under controlled circumstances, according to Dr. Donald B. Louria, President of the New York State Council on Drug Addiction. In a *New York Times Magazine* article of April, 1967, he reports that out of 114 cases treated at Bellevue Hospital in New York City over the pre-ceding 18 months, 13 percent entered in a st-overwhelming panic. In 12 percent of the ca or was uncontrolled violence, and in nea had to cent, there were attempts at eit' suicide. One out of seven of the

be committed for long-term mental hospitalization—
and in half of these cases, there was no prior history
of psychiatric disorder.

The dangers of indiscriminate use to young people
especially should be apparent. Says Dr. Cohen:

"Some of the young in mind who obtain the black
market material will casually take it under dubious
conditions and without the necessary controls. Sooner
or later they will find themselves caught in the grip
of pure horror. With LSD the 'kicks' can go both
ways. Other people will be given LSD without their
knowledge, by design or accident, and will suffer the
shattering belief that they are going mad. A suicide
resulting from such an event has already been described in psychiatric literature. Most of the recent
sufferers from complications whom we studied had
obtained LSD from improper sources."

If any doubt remains as to the kind of dynamite a
person is fooling with when he takes LSD, the following shocking revelation by Dr. Cohen about the
effect of the drug on the psychiatric profession itself
should remove it completely. He reports a "strange
malady" beginning to afflict some psychotherapists
who give LSD to their patients:

"This peculiar disorder might be called *therapist
breakdown.* An unusual number of those dispensing
these drugs have themselves come down with psychiatric disturbances. . . . After intensive, though
sometimes only after brief, contact with the drugs, a
few have gone on to psychotic breakdown or to
megalomaniacal ideas of grandeur. Marked depres-
and even a suicide in which these agents played
so are known. A couple of practitioners have
selves in legal difficulties because of anti-
"

Obviously, this does not apply to the ordinary able psychiatrist who is administering the drug under carefully controlled conditions to properly selected patients. "Nor is therapist breakdown a hazard to the stable physician who uses LSD for his patient's needs, not his own," Dr. Cohen points out.

If all this is not enough to convince your youngster that he is better off to seek his "kicks" elsewhere, perhaps he may be impressed by the little publicized, but quite important possibility, that he may be played for a sucker if he gets caught up in one of the mystical movements. According to a study made of them, *Utopiates,*[1] some appear to be headed by people whose only interest is making money by selling drugs to users and charging for various services; or sexual exploitation; or gratification of the paranoid desire to exercise power over other people. The authors point out that in some instances "naive and well-intentioned organizers are exploited by the psychopathic and cunning ones, just as the latter can go on to exploit patients, clients, parishioners, or anyone else."

In addition, when the drug is administered by non-medical men, it is usually obtained from the black market, and there is no way of knowing just how strong a dose is. If you consider the fact that a few gallons of LSD is enough for everyone in the United States to take one dose, the danger of taking even one drop too many is very apparent.

An explanation of these facts, given by you in a calm and reasonable manner, ought to be e̶r̶s̶e̶r̶s̶ convince your boy or girl not to fool

---

[1] Richard Blum & Associates, *Utopiate of LSD-25;* The Atherton Press, 1964

LSD. But as in the case of marihuana smoking, there could be strong psychological or social reasons why the youngster is drawn to it. If you have any reason to believe that the talk has not been successful, you must not hesitate to ask your physician, a psychologist, or some other informed person for help. It might also be advisable to consult with the school authorities. Naturally, if you detect any unusual behavior, such as extreme depression, fear, or nervousness, take the youngster to the doctor right away.

In one respect, LSD is more dangerous than any other drug. A single dose can cause serious and sometimes irreparable damage. This is so even when the person has taken it a number of times before. Therefore, you must do everything possible to prevent your child from trying it even once, or if he has already taken it, from doing so again.

Similar to LSD in some of its effects and hazards is mescaline, which is the active ingredient in the famous peyote, the dried disk-like tops of the mescal cactus taken by certain American Indians in their religious ceremonials. In its purified form, mescaline produces powerful hallucinations, causes severe fluctuations in mood, and can bring about an agonizing fear of death. A tolerance develops for the drug, so that larger and larger doses are required to produce the hallucinations, but it is not physically habit-forming. As in the case of LSD, mescaline can trigger off a psychotic condition in the person who takes it. The use of peyote itself is virtually confined to the Indians, who are permitted by the United States government to import it from Mexico.

If you have reason to believe that your youngster is around with mescaline or is doing so, you must put a stop to it. Have a talk with him and explain the dangers which are very much the same as those of taking LSD. If the talk is not successful, you must assume that there is an emotional or psychological reason for it, and you should consult with a physician, psychiatrist, or other professional. Of course, if the youngster seems to be very depressed or nervous, take him to the doctor immediately.

Another hallucination producing drug sometimes taken by youngsters is really in a class by itself. This is cocaine, which is often used by doctors and dentists as a local anesthetic. When the flaky, white substance is sniffed or injected (the user heats it in a spoon or vial to liquify it), the drug is a powerful stimulant creating an intense mental exhilaration that usually lasts less than an hour. Not only does the user sometimes hallucinate while under the influence of the drug, but paranoid delusions occasionally continue even after it wears off. Cocaine is not addicting, and unlike in the case of heroin or barbiturates, a tolerance to it is not built up. But it is a very harmful drug. The result of its use is a serious deterioration of the addict's physical and mental faculties. To cut down the intensity of his reaction, the user often adds heroin, forming a mixture called a "speedball."

The symptoms of cocaine use are dilation of the pupils of the eye, unexplainable elation while the person is under the drug's influence, extreme nervousness and vagueness when he is not, loss of weight, a sickly look, and perhaps nonsensical behavior. If you suspect that your youngster has been experimenting with cocaine or actually using it, follow the procedures outlined in the next chapter for what to do if your youngster is taking pills.

8: What to Do If Your Youngster Is Taking Pills

You have seen enough symptoms to suspect that your youngster is taking pills on more than an experimental basis, though you cannot, of course, be certain. He has lost his appetite, he is losing weight, he is slovenly, he seems to be in a daze all the time. You may have found a box of sleeping pills or pep pills hidden in his room.

As you know what the consequences of the use of such drugs can be, you must find out for certain whether he has been taking pills, and if so, for how long, and under what conditions. Therefore, the first thing you do is to have a serious talk with him.

Your approach might be that you are concerned with the possibility that he is in ill-health. You can point out that you have noticed his different behavior and that he doesn't seem to be well at all. He may deny stoutly that there is anything different about him these days, show resentment and irritation. Or he may admit to not feeling well.

In either case, you have to put the question to him —not antagonistically, not accusingly, but in the same spirit of calm, objective concern that any decent parent should feel when he thinks his child is ill: Has he been taking drugs, in particular, pills of one sort or another?

If he has been, hopefully he will tell you so at this point. It is essential now that your response be calm and understanding. You have one objective—to get him to a physician for examination. He should be told that you have to take him to the doctor because you know the drugs cause bodily damage. You hope nothing has happened, but you cannot take a chance.

But the youngster may deny that he has been taking pills. It is not necessary to accuse him of lying, or even to suggest that you intend to check on him through the examination. Your argument is quite sound. If he hasn't been using drugs, wonderful. You are delighted to hear it. However, it is obvious that he has not been feeling well, and you want to find out what is really wrong. Then make the appointment.

Why can't you just believe him and let it go at that, figuring that he's just suffering from growing pains after all? Particularly, if he's always been truthful with you?

Because, regardless of his past sense of honor, *if he has been on drugs for any length of time, he can no longer be trusted to tell the truth—even to you.*

This is virtually impossible for some parents to accept, for it strikes at the heart of their relationship with their children. It suggests to them that they are failures, that the child no longer trusts or respects or loves them. None of this is so. The lying is related to the psychological effect of drug use. He is afraid that he will be deprived of his new crutch. In addition, he may simply be ashamed to admit to you what he has been doing. For his sake, therefore, you cannot be guided by whether you think he is telling the truth or not. Medical evidence agrees that you cannot depend on anyone to tell the truth, once he has become dependent to any degree on drugs. Boiled down to the essential this means, you just cannot take any chances.

It is important that you tell the family physician the truth, because to give a proper examination he must be prepared to look for evidence of drug abuse. This is a reason, incidentally, why you should go to the family physician, if you have one, rather than to a stranger. Many parents are ashamed to go to the doctor they know. They shouldn't be. If you belong to one of the medical group plans, you can talk to the doctor who is normally assigned to you.

When the physician does not feel that he is qualified to make a diagnosis, he will refer you to someone who is. Don't be afraid to ask him directly whether drug abuse is something he is familiar with.

If you don't have a family doctor and do not belong to a group, pick up the phone book and look for the number of the county medical society, which will know those doctors in the area who have been doing work in the narcotics field. Explain that you have no family physician and that you are interested in having a child examined for possible drug abuse. How should you go about it?

There may be some communities in which the medical society is reluctant to make recommendations to a telephoning layman. Should this turn out to be the case when you call, don't be discouraged. Get in touch with your priest, minister, or rabbi and ask him to act for you. He will usually be able to get the information you need.

If all these measures fail, write or call one of the services listed in the appendix of this book.

Do not ask friends, relatives, or any acquaintances for advice, unless there is some reason for you to feel they are well informed in this area.

Before going to the doctor, alert him in advance to the reason for the visit, so that he can allot the required amount of time and prepare himself for the examination, which has two parts:

First, a thorough physical examination.

Second, a careful, probing history, bordering on a psychiatric interview.

Because the latter requires a specific kind of experience and skill, the physician might refer you to a psychiatrist, who will conduct the interview. There will follow a conference or exchange of data between the physician and psychiatrist to determine whether there is a psychological problem or not. They will try to find out whether the youngster is:

1. Merely an experimenter, with little likelihood of going further after some talking to;

2. Emotionally disturbed and in need of treatment for an ailment of which the drug abuse is only a symptom;

3. Seriously disturbed and in need of immediate psychiatric assistance.

If they do conclude that there is a psychological problem, they will recommend one of several possible courses of therapy which are not very different from those employed in the treatment of other conduct disorders in youth. Assuming a still early stage, what will probably be involved is nothing more than some psychiatric counselling. The psychiatrist will attempt to find out such things as: What need is the drug filling? Is there some physical problem, such as obesity or deformity which brings shame to the child? Are there conflicts at home? Is there a lack of respect for the parent? Is the child having difficulty belonging? It's basically a matter of talking things over with the youngster and helping to set him straight. In many cases, such counselling will do the job. But if more treatment is indicated, the psychiatrist will have to determine:

1. Should the psychiatrist treat the boy as a private patient?

2. Should the therapy be applied directly by the physician, once he has the findings and recommendations of the psychiatrist?

3. Is the best place for treatment in a hospital, social agency, or clinic? If this is the case, he will have to consider what facilities are available in your community and whether it would be necessary to go elsewhere for help, even to another state.

4. Is drug therapy indicated?

It is clear that difficult and delicate decisions have to be made. The problems are tough enough for the professionals to cope with. It would be a mistake for you to try to compete with them. Moreover, the young person expects you to bring up unpleasant things, and he may resent it, thus making it difficult for you to influence him. When you call in the physician and psychiatrist, you are providing your youngster with figures of authority that command his respect, and at the same time you are demonstrating in an unmistakable way that you are truly concerned, that you care deeply. Often, this can be the beginning of a dramatic change for the better.

This must be emphasized even though we know that the medical men themselves do not have all of the answers. Nevertheless, their abilities are the best we have at this time, and we can do no better than to rely on their judgment, skill and dedication. With their assistance, we have a real chance. Without it, and blundering along by ourselves, we have very little.

9: What to Do If Your Youngster Is Taking Heroin or One of the Other Opiates

You have found evidence—the hypodermic and the homemade cooker, perhaps a bag of heroin as well. There are suspicious scars or scabs on the youngster's arms or on the back of his hands. He has been disappearing for long periods of time, and has been seen with questionable companions in seedy places. You know you cannot just sit back and wait.

In order to understand clearly what you must do and why you must do it, keep in mind the terrible ways heroin use affects a person physically and psychologically. Let us review them:

1. The youngster finds through experimentation that the heroin offers him a way of escaping temporarily from his tensions and responsibilities.

2. He finds that he has to keep increasing the dose of the drug, because the body builds up a tolerance and it takes larger and larger amounts to achieve the desired effect.

3. When the effect of the heroin wears off, physical and mental agony sets in, and the victim must obtain the drug in order to stop the torment. Not very long after he takes another dose, the effect begins to wear off, the turmoil starts again, and he has to set out once more to obtain the drug in order to get some relief. So he finds himself having to inject four or five shots of heroin a day.

4. Since it is against the law to possess or sell heroin, it can only be obtained from underworld sources at a very high price. But the average youngster cannot afford the large sums of money needed every day, so he inevitably winds up either stealing or selling drugs to others— that is, becoming a "pusher" himself. The female addict usually turns to prostitution.

5. To obtain the drug, the user will not only break the law, he will lie and deceive anyone, even those closest to him. He is immune to reason and appeals to his conscience.

6. The drug takes him over. He lives only to get his four or five shots for the day—every day. Obtaining and using the heroin consumes all his energies. Nothing else really matters, or even exists. He is unaware of the world around him. His friends will be other heroin users.

7. Sooner or later, the addict will be arrested

for thievery or, in the case of a girl, prostitution, and will begin a tortured essentially futile round of trials, imprisonments, and hospital treatments. In all of this, his or her family is enmeshed and there is an endless circle of misery for all.

8. Often an accidental, or subconsciously intentional, overdose brings an early death.

The same process of addiction and the same horrible effects on a person's mind and body result from the misuse of other drugs that, like heroin, are derived from opium—such as morphine, dilaudid, codeine, and paregoric. Probably the best known of these is morphine, which is prescribed by doctors to relieve pain and mental anxiety. It is not as powerful as heroin, but because pushers and addicts obtain it by stealing from doctors' offices and drug warehouses and by forging prescriptions, a dose is usually much purer and thus more potent than an equal amount of heroin, which is ordinarily diluted by the black-marketeer. Dilaudid, a pain killer also used legitimately in medicine, is five times as powerful as morphine, but it is considerably rarer, so it is usually not involved in the drug-abuse pattern. Codeine and paregoric, on the other hand, are comparatively mild and quite common. The former is often prescribed to relieve coughing and kill pain, and paregoric is often given to stop diarrhea and stomach cramps. It takes a great deal of these to build up an addiction, but it is possible and does happen.. Then, of course, there is opium itself, the most romanticized of the drugs. Although never as important in this country as the fiction of yesterday made it out to be, it is still smoked by some people. Finally, there is a synthetic drug, meperdine —or Demerol, as it is popularly known— which has effects very much like morphine. For all practical purposes, the discussion about what to do if your youngster is using heroin applies to any of the opiates or Demerol.

Now, what do you do if you suspect that your child is experimenting with or using heroin? There is only one thing you can do: You must assume that he is using the drug and act accordingly. You have no other choice at this stage. *You must act on this assumption, hoping it will finally turn out to be false.*

Your immediate task is to get him to a doctor. If he denies that he has been taking the drug, tells you that the hypodermic and the narcotic are not his but someone else's, or that the pin pricks and scars have some other cause, just remember what has been said about the drug user's readiness to lie to those closest to him. You have to insist that he go for an examination anyway. Explain that it's not in order to check up on his story, but because you are worried about his general condition. If he admits that he has been using it and agrees to cooperate with you, find out exactly how frequently he takes it, how large the doses are, and what withdrawal symptoms he has. This information will be a great help to the doctor.

When you make the appointment be sure to tell the doctor the purpose of the visit so that he can arrange for a very thorough examination to be given under the proper condition. In addition to his own examination he will want others by qualified specialists. If he does not know what local facilities are available, he will get in touch with his county medical society or the Mental Health Association in the area to find out.

An important part of the examination is psychiatric. It consists of interviews with the youngster and you to determine what in his emotional make-up is being satisfied by taking narcotics, and what factors in his home life and environment are predisposing him to the use of drugs. Again, it is important to distinguish between the three phases:

1. *Experimentation.*
2. *Building dependence.*
3. *Dependence, or addiction.*

While addiction frequently takes hold very shortly after initiation, there are also many cases in which it builds slowly. Sometimes the young person is what is known as a "weekend" user, who indulges in the drug infrequently or at regular intervals over a rather long period of time. Dependence builds up more slowly, but it does come about.

No one maintains that the process of addiction is easy to reverse. It isn't. But the chances are better at the earlier stages than at the later one. Before the craving has become overwhelming, before the drug has taken over the person entirely, it is often still possible to reach the victim, to provide him with the therapy that will help to direct his interest away from the escape seemingly provided by heroin to constructive patterns of development. As Dr. Louria writes: "To be effective, a rehabilitation program must reach addicts in their teens or early twenties."

The trouble is, that when you discover that your child is a possible heroin user, you have no way of knowing how far he has actually gone along the road, regardless of what he tells you. In study after study of addiction appear shocking cases of parents who do not find out that their youngster is an addict for several years, by which time he is probably utterly enslaved by the drug. This is one reason why you must assume the worst and take action without delay.

If the addiction is not fully developed, it may be possible to detoxify the youngster outside a hospital and to handle his treatment pretty much the same way one deals with another kind of ambulatory patient. It all depends on how early one catches the condition and the nature of the case. Treatment then will involve visits to the psychotherapist, a clinic, or a social agency, with continued counselling and frequent medical checking. It may even be that detoxification in the normal sense is unnecessary if the youngster has been experimenting or has not yet gone far enough in his occasional use of heroin to develop the so-called abstinence syndrome, that is, the effects of withdrawal. If, on the other hand, dependence has developed, your job is to get the youngster to submit himself to a comprehensive course of treatment and rehabilitation—without delay. This may mean immediate hospitalization, or semi-hospitalization with treatment in a clinic, part of which is purely medical, involving detoxification or withdrawal, and part psychological. It all depends on the nature of the case and the individual circumstances. No one answer works for all cases.

We now come to the most difficult of all the problems that a parent may have to face. *Your son refuses to go for treatment. He refuses even to go for an examination. What do you do?*

What are the alternatives open to you? The first is to accept the boy's refusal and simply try to live with his use of drugs. There's a very simple reason why you cannot do this. It will inevitably lead to disaster.

Recall the description of the course of heroin addiction given earlier. It is clear how the process, if allowed to go unchecked, feeds upon itself and leads to full addiction with all that means. *If you accept his refusal to be examined or treated or both, you are accepting that tragedy. You are giving up at the beginning.*

You should try over a period of days, perhaps a couple of weeks, to persuade the boy to cooperate, for a great deal of unpleasant and heartbreaking experience may possibly be avoided. Still, you may not succeed. At this point it would be advisable to ask someone else to help you convince the boy, perhaps a minister or rabbi or your family physician, someone who understands what is involved and who can serve as a figure of authority to back up your demands.

Indeed, it may very well be the wisest course to enlist the aid of a professional person of this sort at the beginning. It is a tough situation even for the most controlled of people. You may be well advised to talk with your family physician, priest, rabbi, or minister, to confide in him and ask for his assistance before confronting the youngster.

It is worth making a very serious effort to win the cooperation of your child. But if all efforts fail, if no matter how hard all of you try, he still won't agree, and you can look forward only to his continuing and increasing use of the drug, then you have to face the question whether you should force him to take treatment.

You must be very clear in your own mind what this means. It means that you are going to use the law. *Ultimately, the law is the only real club you have in this situation.*

This does not mean that you should have him arrested. It means that you should take advantage of whatever legal machinery exists in your community to force the youngster to submit to treatment without involving him in the unpleasant and difficult business of arrest and imprisonment.

While there is no uniform law on these matters throughout the country, more and more states are adopting procedures for the forced commitment of a person for a course of treatment without his being given a criminal record. In those states, the young person who is brought to the authorities as an addict is offered the opportunity to undergo treatment instead of going to jail. If he chooses the treatment there is no entry on any kind of police record, so he can escape that stigma.

In California and New York, if the addict does not wish to cooperate, it no longer matters, for the law now says that he has to undergo treatment as determined by an appropriate board of physicians and in a place which the board decides on. He becomes a ward of the state for quite a long time. Prospects for passage of a Federal law that will provide for such civil commitment on a national basis are favorable.

It may not be necessary to go this far. In some communities the juvenile court may be the best place to start. Often it will be enough for the judge, when apprised of the situation, to confront the youngster with the choices open to him, thus convincing him before action is taken that he really would do best to comply with the wishes of his parents.

As every county has its own local ordinances, no universal rule can be given for the parent to follow. You must find out what the nature of the legal machinery is in your community before you start any action. This is another reason why it makes a great deal of sense to work together with your physician or minister who, if he himself does not know the answer, at least knows how to find out where to go for the necessary information. He can then advise you.

Your last resort, if nothing else works, is the law. You have to be very careful, however, that you understand exactly how the law works where you live. For example, it will do your child no good to have him arrested in a community which has no facilities for treatment and where the usual practice is to toss addicts into jail. Unfortunately, in most of the country the addict is still considered a criminal rather than a sick person, and is treated accordingly. Often your best chance is to get in touch with your district or county attorney's office where your cooperation will be valued and where there will probably be much greater interest in dealing with the drug problem than in punishing your child. If your youngster should go to court, a sympathetic recommendation from the district attorney's office can mean a great deal to his future.

To have the youngster committed for treatment against his will is, of course, very difficult for most parents. They feel that they are being cruel to their own flesh and blood and that they are casting the child out. How can the youngster understand what is really involved? How can he feel anything but that his parents have betrayed him and abandoned him? There is much confusion inside a parent at such a moment. Often he feels guilty for having somehow failed the child; he blames himself for what has happened. He cannot even be sure that he may not simply be trying to relieve himself of an onerous burden. And so the parent is tempted not to go through with it, to grab once more at the straw of hope that perhaps through his own efforts and loving care, he can achieve the miracle which will make the commitment unnecessary.

No one can lay down the rules for such a situation. No one has the right to say "do thus" and "thus." And in truth, there is another side to the question.

Many experts believe that it is impossible to treat an addict successfully unless he wants to be rehabilitated, and that, therefore, compulsory treatment is doomed at the start. This is an easy argument to accept if you are ridden with guilt feelings and find you do not have the stomach to set the legal machinery in motion. The difficulty with this point of view is that it allows no way to attack the youngster's problems if he is not willing to cooperate. From a practical standpoint, it means consigning the youngster to an addict's fate.

Those who take the position that you must act argue that regardless of the difficulty of working with an unwilling patient, there is at least a chance he will be helped along the way, and that some chance is better than none. Moreover, it is sometimes possible to obtain good results even when the addict starts the treatment program full of antagonism.

The views of Dr. Marc Kenyon, Executive Director of the Nassau County Medical Society, are representative of what most experts think:

"You are not able to enforce your demand as a parent, yet you know that without any treatment, your child will become a public charge eventually. So this isn't a matter of medical, but legal prophylaxis. You have no recourse except to get in touch with whatever agency operates in your community. You should find out what the legal steps are in your community, and how you can work within the law. I am not suggesting that you call the police or the narcotics squad. Basically your objective is not to seek retribution or punishment, but to find a way to start a program of rehabilitation without destroying any of the potentials you hope to realize.

"In this county, for example, I'd get in touch with the juvenile court after getting the diagnosis and recommendation for treatment by the family physician and whatever specialist or agency he works with. The parent can then make the child a ward of the court, which will then determine the course of treatment. I would rather reconcile myself to this than to a greater loss later on. It is not a pleasant decision.

"Is it worth taking the risk? The only analogy I can give you is a known malignancy or leukemia. Do we say, what's the use, we can't cure it, and let the person die? We've got to try. Maybe this person will be part of the small percentage who can be rehabilitated. Even six months of normal life is better than absolute dissolution.

"There is always the rebound, soul-searching as to whether the decision was correct. But when you finally face the situation, what else can you do? Shall you deny your responsibility as a parent and say, all right, go along your way? He will be arrested anyway as a junkie."

Why does Dr. Kenyon say he will be a public ward anyway? The reason is that the heroin addict is inevitably arrested either for violating the narcotics laws or for some criminal act resulting from his need for money. The record shows that the average addict is picked up by the police after two years of being on the drug.

The difficulties inherent in the problem are seen, perhaps, in the simple fact that despite all that has been said about avoiding entanglements with the police if you can help it, there are still times when even a prison sentence may appear preferable to the hopeless and dangerous life of the addict. Even ministers are now being educated to these harsh realities. As Tommie L. Duncan, the chaplain director of the Federal narcotics hospital at Fort Worth, Texas, states, in a book written to instruct pastors on how to handle the narcotics addict: "Finally, and this is a last resort (no other alternatives being available) the addict can be withdrawn in jail. Sometimes families who feel unable to control the addict, and believe that eventually he will hurt himself, call authorities to take the addict into custody. For the minister, I would suggest this method only if no other solution seems possible."[1]

Father Duncan emphasizes one of the dangers threatening the addict and which the parent must consider when he is debating whether to take legal action. It is the possibility of taking an overdose. How many young people die each year because of overdoses no one knows, but there is reason to believe the number is shockingly high. Most of the time the user does not know how much heroin is actually in the shot. The doses, remember, are obtained illegally through a network of pushers who are notorious for diluting what they sell, and the addict might assume the shot is less potent than it is. Or the user may misjudge his tolerance for the drug. Sometimes the same self-destructive tendency

---

[1] Tommie L. Duncan, *Understanding and Helping the Narcotic Addict*, Prentice-Hall, 1965.

that has caused a person to become an addict in the first place, leads him consciously or unconsciously to take an overdose.

Often also, the addict becomes ill because of his rundown condition brought on by the drug usage. Death may ensue from a great many diseases.

There is another consideration. As time goes on, life with the addict becomes impossible for the family. Because of his compulsion and the all-encompassing nature of the addiction, he cannot function normally as a family member. He has no sense of responsibility, is incapable of maintaining a job or going to school, cannot be relied on to carry out tasks or keep appointments. The family never knows when he is telling the truth or when he is lying. It must constantly be on the alert for possible stealing, regardless of the addict's expressed good intentions. Because of his associations in the drug world, he is likely to get into trouble frequently and his parents can anticipate frequent visits to the court or even jail. Arguments are endless and meaningless.

The addict quickly becomes skillful in fooling his parents into thinking that he is reforming and in obtaining money from them by a multitude of ruses. They, in turn, find themselves drained financially as well as emotionally. The amount of money that can go down this bottomless drain is astonishing. Families have been known to mortgage their homes and businesses to no avail. There is no end to the demands of the drug.

And so, at some point, possibly after many years of such existence, the parents come to realize that the situation is intolerable. A breaking point is reached. There is no alternative but to throw the addict out of the house. Perhaps, the parents con-.

sole themselves, when he has reached bottom and there are no more crutches left for him to lean on, he will then seek out treatment.

If this seems extreme, be assured that it is commonplace. Indeed, to throw the addict out of the house, is more often than one might think the advice given to parents by professionals who see that the futile pattern of existence has been maintained too long for either the welfare of the addict or the family.

A rabbi who worked together with a priest in an institution devoted to treatment for addiction, received a telephone call from a woman. She reported that her son was taking drugs again. What should she do? The rabbi replied: "Have him arrested, and have him thrown out of the house."

The Reverend Gallagher of the Catholic Charities Narcotic Unit tells about a mother who came to him with her addicted son, who was twenty years old. He had been stealing everything out of the house. There were four younger children. The neighbors and the landlord were up-in-arms over the boy's behavior. Reverend Gallagher told her she had no choice. She had to consider the rest of the family. Even though it seemed very cruel, he said the boy had to go.

Moving the family to another neighborhood or town in the hope of solving the problem is futile. If you go, say, to a farm in Iowa, that might indeed be helpful. There is a very short supply of narcotics in the rural areas of the Midwest, so whatever emotional disturbances prompted the drug usage in the first place would have to find some other form of expression. Transplanting from one city to another, though, will probably accomplish nothing. Wherever the addict goes he can find another addict and a source of supply. And if one moves from the center of the city to a suburban area, there is no way of preventing the youngster from going into the city to obtain the drug. There are cases, many of them, of families selling their homes, moving to other states, finding that nothing changes, and returning to start all over again. Furthermore, sending a youngster away into a more favorable environment is itself a form of treatment and should not be done unless a physician or psychiatrist advises it.

In the final analysis, you have no choice but to force the youngster to undergo treatment by whatever means are necessary, even if, as a last resort, you have to turn him over to the police. The alternative is his destruction and very possibly your own. To sum up the reasons:

1. Drug dependence will not go away by itself. If left to its own natural course it will almost certainly turn into full addiction.

2. The addict will sooner or later run afoul of the law, become a public charge, and be forced to undergo some form of treatment anyway but under difficult, harsh, tragic circumstances.

3. Family life is virtually impossible with an addict. Perhaps after years of all kinds of troubles, the youngster will have to be forced out of the house.

4. Moving to another neighborhood or city will not as a rule, make any difference.

5. The end of the road for the addict is often a miserable death from an overdose or disease.

The sooner you act, the better will be the youngster's chance for recovery. The longer you delay, the greater will be the torment suffered by him and by you. If you let guilt feelings or pride, instead of reason, govern your decisions, you are inviting catastrophe.

10: The Price of Pride

One of the major culprits in the narcotics tragedy is pride.

It is pride which delays action until it is almost too late. It is pride which says, it can happen to your son and his or her son, but not to mine. It is pride which says, my child will not succumb, cannot succumb, my child is better than yours.

It is a dangerous pride.

The simple fact is that most parents are not prepared to admit even to themselves that the narcotics epidemic can affect them and their families. We have been fed for so many decades on the myth of the dope fiend that we react not with intelligence but with shock when even the possibility of addiction strikes close to home. Our reaction tends to be so emotional as to make sensible action almost impossible. We struggle with feelings of shame, and we worry about what the neighbors will think, about how the youngster's behavior will threaten what we have accomplished with our hard work and our status in the community, when we should be thinking clearly about how best to help him.

Too often, indeed, these deep-seated feelings of shame lead the parent to "blackout" the facts that are clearly pointing to addiction. In our hearts we simply cannot believe that our own child can be doing these things we have always believed so evil.

And so we close our eyes to the truth. We may see all the signs and know enough to interpret them correctly—yet we refuse to recognize what they point to.

This point is so basic, so important, that it must be stressed again and again. If you do not recognize it, everything that is said in this book concerning the evidence of drug use and how to interpret the telltale signs will have no meaning, for psychologically you will find the whole situation so unpleasant, that when the times comes for action, you may be paralyzed and do nothing until too late.

You may be thinking, "No, I am not like that. I can face the truth even if it involves my own child." Hopefully, you are right. The fact is however, that most of us are so deeply involved emotionally with our children, that we of all people have the most trouble in being objective about their growth problems. This is the case when we are trying to cope with the normal puzzles of adolescent behavior. How much more difficult it is to be objective when something so terrifying as possible drug addiction suddenly confronts us!

Be warned: However normal and excellent your relationship with your child may be, however sensible you think you will be should the drug threat appear, there is a fair chance that you may actually delude yourself into thinking that nothing is happening.

This may be a difficult concept for you to accept at this point. What is important is that you remember it is a possibility and that you make a deliberate effort to question whether you are acting as objectively as you think. There is, after all, a very good reason why lawyers challenge the right of people to sit on a jury when they have some relationship with one of the principals in a trial. They may become emotionally involved, even when they do not think they will.

For many parents "addiction is simply too great a shock for them to cope with," says a social worker in the New York City Office of the Narcotics Coordinator. "They say, 'I'm imagining things. Am I accusing wrongly?' They won't accept the addiction until they absolutely have to." He tells the story of a policeman whose son took an overdose of narcotics and had to go to the hospital. "The policeman kept insisting it was an accident. He found addiction in his son impossible to accept, and was in a state of shock. Later he admitted, 'I'd have known what to do if someone who was an addict walked into the station.'"

Then there is the quite common case of the overindulgent mother who is the last in the neighborhood to know that her son is addicted. She is so busy giving in to him she doesn't inquire into what is happening. She doesn't see the money he is taking, she's not aware he is pawning their clothing. Before she finally faces reality, the household property has been stolen. Sometimes, she will continue to deny his addiction after he is actually arrested.

The Reverend Lynn Hegemann, head of Exodus House, a narcotics clinic in Harlem, says: "The parents first avoid dealing with the problem, then refuse to recognize it." He cites the case of a mother who has an inkling that her son is on drugs, but refuses to admit he is taking them. She finds all sorts of reasons to drop extra money in his lap. She accepts all his explanations for not working or going to school. She never really questions him. She may nag, but will do nothing else. "This can go on for as long as three to four years, and it is as true in the suburbs as it is in the city."

At a meeting of addicts and the mothers of addicts held at Samaritan Half-Way House in Queens, New York, a number of startling examples of the "blocking" action were met with. One woman who is an addict together with her husband (he was out on bail at this point) reported that neither her own parents nor those of her husband were even yet aware of their addiction. And this was in spite of the signs, such as falling weight, strange behavior, and the like. The families "knew" the truth, she believed, but could not admit it, even to themselves.

Another startling case was cited to the author by a school psychologist. The boy was using seconal. He did not get up for school. His mother woke him. He seemed groggy, almost in a coma.

"What's the matter?" his mother asked.

"Nothing," was the reply.

She helped him to dress and guided him to the breakfast table. While she was serving him breakfast, he slipped off his chair. Once more she questioned him. Once more he said there was nothing wrong. She accepted his assurance, despite the obvious signs. On the surface, the youngster may have tried to look assured; inside he was sick and scared.

She drove him to school, though normally he would have walked, deposited him on the steps, and drove away. In her car's rear-view mirror she saw that he had fallen down, unable to support himself. Nevertheless, she continued on her way to work.

Two friends of his took him to his English class. As soon as the teacher saw and talked with him, she called for the school psychologist, who shortly afterwards started to work with the boy and his mother.

During their meeting, the psychologist asked the mother: "When you saw the boy fall on the school steps, why didn't you turn back? Why did you continue to drive on?"

Her answer was pathetic. "I had to go to work."

But the real reason was that she did not want to admit to herself that her boy was using drugs.

Of course, this is an extreme case. It does happen though, because drug addiction strikes at the roots of our fears, and as a result we are often quick to erect mental barriers to understanding when the problem arises in our own family.

Perhaps the usual reaction by a parent is a wretched sense of guilt. Not only does he feel that something shameful is occurring, he also feels that he has failed in some important respect as a parent —otherwise, how could his child have gone wrong? The addiction is seen as a virtual statement that all his efforts as a parent have been in vain. He interprets the child's behavior as a total rejection; the youngster seems to be saying to him, "To show you how I really feel, I am willing even to destroy myself!" For this the parent blames himself and is often afraid that others—relatives, friends, the community —will blame him too.

Some parents, while not particularly blaming themselves, delay taking action because they worry about exposing the youngster and themselves to the social stigma resulting from an old-fashioned public attitude. They are afraid that the youngster will be looked upon as a criminal instead of as someone suffering from a serious disease and that he and his family will be shamed.

Such is the depth of the emotions released, that families will go to great lengths to keep the addiction hidden. Often the parents will try everything they can to prevent relatives from knowing the truth. If they have money they will, after sending the youngster to a private hospital or sanitorium, explain to friends and relatives that he is on a trip or away at school. They may send him to some other city to live, or to Europe.

Sometimes they will not even be able to talk to their family doctor, who is most likely to be in a position to give immediate help, but will go to some strange doctor instead. There are cases where the parents are unable to face their minister when he might be the best source of guidance and counsel. And frequently when they seek help they try to protect their name by sending a relative or trusted friend to talk to a doctor or social agency.

None of this is lost on the youngster. He tends to feel bitter because of his parents' concern with things that are really not essential rather than with his problem. This gets in the way of his rehabilitation.

Pride also frequently interferes with a youngster's recovery in another way. In the final analysis, proper treatment of the addict involves treatment of the family. The young person seeks out drugs at least in part because something is lacking in what he gets from his home. His actions are the result of a life's history, his day-to-day relationships with his parents, as well as with his friends and community. For treatment to succeed, the relations between parents and child must be analyzed and, in all probability, changed.

This is the point at which the average parent balks. He cannot quite accept himself as someone who needs "treatment" along with his addicted youngster. He comes to the doctor, hospital, or agency wanting the *child* taken care of, freed from drugs and restored again, but rejects passionately the idea that *he,* the parent, should become part of the treatment process himself. This, say the professionals, is probably their most difficult problem.

The Reverend Edward Brown of the Lower East Side Information and Youth Center and co-author of the book *Mainline to Nowhere,* cites an extreme example:

"A mother wants someone to magically save her son from the needle. She goes around to a judge, a lawyer, an agency to provide this magical cure. She is not willing to take the steps necessary. She wants the boy to be just as dependent and withdrawn, as passive and scared of the world. When you start working with her to help him get out of the cycle, the whole thing falls apart."

Often it is the adoring, over-protective mother who has the most difficult time understanding and accepting her role in the process which ultimately produced an addict. She has done everything in her power to shelter and control her boy, and now, feeling attacked, her guilt enveloping her, she violently rejects the idea that she herself may have been one of the major factors leading to her son's condition. The record is filled with such cases.

However, fathers even more than mothers, tend to resist participating in the process of treatment, perhaps because they feel the whip of failure more strongly. Reverend Brown's group has tried everything—casework, group therapy, social action groups, recreation groups, field trips—but they haven't been able to get the fathers involved. Fathers have a tendency to write a boy off, so deep are the feelings of guilt and failure.

An agency psychologist tells of a fourteen-year-old boy who seemed to him to be on the way to becoming a drug user. Try as he would, he says, he could not make real contact with the father, a pharmacist, or the mother, a teacher. The psychologist presented his diagnosis to the parents. They refused to accept it. "They cry out their impotent rage and anger, but they cannot verbalize such rage, and until they can, nothing can be done for them." He asked them to undergo treatment. The mother wanted to know for whom would it be cheaper, herself or her husband. No treatment was undertaken.

Dr. Henry Mieselas, Director of the Narcotics Program of the New York State Department of Mental Hygiene, reports that when parents come into his office at Manhattan State Hospital to discuss their youngster's problem and he outlines to them what is involved in a proper course of family treatment, they often balk and reject the idea completely.

Yet, in the long run there is no choice. If the youngster is to be prevented from turning into a full-blown addict, or rehabilitated if addiction has struck, he must find a new source of comfort and identity within his own family, and this will probably not be possible unless his parents undergo therapy along with him.

Elizabeth Goddard, a highly experienced welfare worker who leads mothers of addicts in a group discussion at Samaritan Half-Way House in Corona, New York, explains the importance of treating parents:

"In the beginning, parents are irresponsible. They

claim that they have played no part in their child's addiction. But as they get more and more involved in therapy, they become more inclined to accept the role that they have played. They are still over-protective of their sons. They make the argument that they have given them everything that they could want in a material way. A common pattern is the domineering mother who won't let her child grow up. She is the boss in the house, though she won't admit it. *When these parents really begin to change, their kids change along with them. The parents begin to take more responsibility for their own acts.*"

Most of the addicts do not have a good image of their fathers. The father often appears to be the less dominant of the parents, or because he is absent a good deal he is often little more than a shadow about the house, and the children hardly know him. Miss Goddard tells of the case of the family in which the father was holding two jobs in order to earn enough money to move his family out of the city into a house in the suburbs. He thought he was doing the best thing for his son. But the youngster began to use drugs. When this was brought to his attention and it was made clear to him that from the youngster's point of view his absence was seen as abandonment rather than as help, he quit his second job so that he would have more time to spend with his child. This was the beginning of a change in the boy's behavior. The story ended happily.

Probation workers and school administrators report the same experience. They have noticed that where the parents have understood the need for them to participate in the treatment along with the youngster, good results have often been achieved. This is particularly true, they point out, in the early teen years, when the youngster is just beginning to use drugs. The willingness of the mother and father to sit down and discuss the family situation openly and air problems concerning their relationship with their offspring, is often enough to show the youngster that they really care and that they are interested in doing whatever is necessary to improve the relationship between them. In this way they are answering his cry for love, and he responds.

One point should, perhaps, be made clear. The fact that you may require some kind of "treatment" along with your youngster does not mean that you are being accused of doing something wrong or of having been stupid, mistaken, or foolish in the way you brought up the child. It has always been difficult to raise children. The perfect child-parent relationship is rare, if not impossible. From day to day, we all try to do our best. We cannot always know when things are going wrong.

It is in no sense a disgrace for a family to sit down with a therapist, a social worker, or a physician. On the contrary it indicates an intelligent and mature awareness of the problems, as well as admirable objectivity and self-discipline.

The parent should not make the mistake of attempting his own diagnosis. As Dr. Henry Brill points out: "Trying to practice psychiatry and psychology with a layman's point of view and a layman's knowledge of it is more misleading than constructive."

Time after time, there turns out to be a "silent curtain" separating children and parents, says the Reverend David Wilkinson, who runs Teen Challenge. In virtually every case of addiction there is a breakdown in communication. It is the job of the professional to help the family pull aside the silent curtain and begin to communicate with one another. But ultimately it is not the professional, but the family itself which must actually open that curtain.

11: The Treatment of Drug Addiction

• *There are no miracle cures—don't waste your time looking for them.*

• *Your doctor cannot get rid of addiction by writing out a prescription, by giving your youngster a pill or shot.*

• *The psychotherapy fashioned to cope with the usual neuroses is meaningless, and the psychoanalyst is generally helpless.*

• *There are no super-specialists who have the magic touch, so it is futile to search for one as you might hunt for a great surgeon.*

• *You are inviting disaster if you go to hypnotists, chiropractors, or others on the fringe of medicine, however valuable you may regard their skills where other conditions are concerned.*

• *Money makes no significant difference in securing better or more rapid treatment; at most, it might enable the patient to enjoy some personal comfort.*

Please don't squander your money on vain searches for magic remedies. You will only wind up disillusioned and bankrupt. An eminent researcher in the narcotics field, Leon Brill, in his report on a five-year community experiment conducted by the New York Demonstration Center, writes that "caseworkers heard seemingly incredible accounts of how fathers with modest means had spent their lives' savings or gone into debt in an impulsive effort to deal with a particular crisis created by the addict. Mr. L., a taxi-driver, financed a three-week private hospital stay for his son at a cost of over $1,000, believing that a more expensive treatment resource would assure a more permanent cure. Mr. P. went to the extreme of taking his son to a doctor in the state of Washington, merely on the basis of a newspaper article describing a new miracle drug, only to have the son return to heroin immediately after arriving back home."

You must understand at the outset that when you start on the road of treatment you are going on a long, winding, difficult journey, which will most likely have several or many detours, and which will take years to complete. If you can think in terms of a chronic disease, you may be able to teach yourself to be patient and to retain whatever degree of sympathetic detachment a parent can be capable of. Both patience and detachment are essential.

But let us get something straight:

No matter what you may hear about the high percentages of relapse, no matter how often you may hear it said that "once a junkie, always a junkie," *the facts are that good results are often obtained; many addicts are successfully rehabilitated, while others make a pretty fair adjustment to life even if they never become completely free of drug use.*

Treatment has two basic aspects, the physical and the emotional.

Withdrawing the addict from heroin—that is, stopping the physiological craving for the drug—does not present any special difficulties today. This can be done in a hospital, a clinic, even at home. Hospital treatment usually involves the use of the drug methadone, which is given orally on a daily basis in decreasing amounts. It is used as a substitute for the narcotic until the addict's system is cleansed. The withdrawal process usually takes about four days, although for heavily addicted persons it may take seven to ten days.

At some institutions no drugs at all are used in withdrawal. The addict goes through the experience in a normal, living-room setting, with others keeping an eye on him and making him comfortable as needed, much as they would treat a friend who is at a party with a very bad cold.

Withdrawal sometimes takes place at home, depending on the degree of addiction and the ability of the family to function sympathetically and intelligently.

Withdrawal from heroin is often a less fearsome ordeal than is suggested by the average description of it, particularly when drawn by the addict. Yes, it is painful, there is discomfort, distress, nausea, running nose. But these things happen with the flu or a heavy cold. The myth has been built largely by the addict's dramatic performances, which are characterized by violent contortions, grimaces, and moans, usually calculated to convince parents and physicians that he is in desperate need of his drug.

The distress of withdrawal has declined in recent years because of the diminishing strength of the shots the heroin user takes. Not that he wants a weak mixture, he usually can't get any other. Federal and local law enforcement has been vigorous during the past few years, and the supply of heroin smuggled into this country has declined. With demand high, the distributors on this end of the supply route dilute the heroin powder with sugar and chemicals. The average heroin shot, as a result, is estimated to be about one-fifth as strong as it was fifteen or twenty years ago. Consequently, the physical hold of the heroin on its victim tends to be less.

But withdrawal from sleeping pills is another matter. It can be dangerous. The U.S. Public Health Service warns: "Sudden, complete withdrawal of barbiturates from an addicted person usualy results in convulsions and often a temporary psychosis resembling delirium tremens. Death may follow. So the drugs must be withdrawn under medical supervision over a relatively long period."[1]

You can see why the Public Health Service says that barbiturates "give the individual and his physician even greater problems than does heroin." The country at large is still not really aware of the terrible dangers associated with the addicting power of the sleeping pill.

Obviously, these dangers must be kept in mind when treatment is undertaken. Because of the growing tendency for addicts to use more than one drug, the problem of withdrawal has become more complicated. The Public Health Service reports:

[1] *Facts about Narcotic Drug Addiction*, U.S. Dept. of Health, Education and Welfare.

"Among the patients at Lexington, the Federal hospital at Lexington, Kentucky, roughly 20 percent have been addicted to both barbiturates and narcotics, and for these, the withdrawal period usually runs from ten to fourteen days. In some cases of addiction to barbiturates, however, withdrawal may take as long as two months."

Under no conditions, should barbiturate withdrawal be attempted at home without medical supervision. The patient's place is generally in a hospital.

Once the addict has been gotten off the drug, once the craving has been removed from his body and he has been made physically healthy—the real work begins.

The most difficult treatment is of the *personality,* of the emotional base of the condition. Until the personality disorder at the root of the drug use is corrected, the craving remains and the victim is subject to relapse.

Less and less does one hear of "cure," more and more of "rehabilitation." In the words of Dr. Efrim Ramirez, Narcotics Program Coordinator of New York City, the addict leads a "sick way of life." The aim of therapy is to enable him to live a healthy way of life. This calls for a total attack: preparation for treatment, physical withdrawal, psychotherapeutic treatment to reach the root cause of his personality disturbance, preparation for "reentry" into the community through counselling, development of attitudes and vocational skills, and aftercare treatment in the years following release from formal treatment. It is a long, tough job.

Unfortunately, there are no institutions or agencies in the United States yet truly able to provide such comprehensive treatment, although serious beginnings have been made in some areas, such as New York State. You must remember that our society is just now organizing itself to grapple with this problem. Until very recently, there were no treatment facilities at all in most states. Only in the past half-dozen years or so has there been any significant improvement in the situation either on the government or private level. Moreover, very few physicians have had experience with or training in the treatment of drug abuse, and full-scale research has only recently begun. It will be a long time before there will be sufficient hospital space to take care of all addicts, and the medical profession is far from agreeing on what the best treatment is.

This is why when you are considering how to handle your youngster's problem, you have to weigh very carefully whether he belongs in a hospital at all. Remember he is still at a highly impressionable age. If he is in the earlier stages of the addictive process there is usually no strong reason to put him in a hospital or other institution. In fact, the reverse is ordinarily the case; there is every reason to keep him out. In a narcotics hospital the young person is thrown into the company of confirmed addicts. That he will come away from the experience a confirmed addict himself, wise in the way of drug procurement and use, is likely. He may also pick up a few hints on how to live a criminal existence. Addicts in hospitals are notorious for passing the time by sharing such information with each other.

However, this is not to say that there are no good hospitals and that good treatment facilities are utterly lacking.

Among the best hospitals in the country are the Federal centers at Lexington, Kentucky, (established in 1938) and Ft. Worth, Texas, (established in 1935), which are run by the National Institute of Mental Health (NIMH). It is at these centers that most of the standard practices of withdrawal care and rehabilitation have been developed, under the supervision of a dedicated staff of world-famous physicians and researchers. For many years they were virtually the only places in the United States an addict could go to for treatment. Today, they are particularly important to those areas in the country which have no facilities of their own. Lexington accepts male addicts east of the Mississippi, Ft. Worth those west. Minors are admitted to Lexington, but only with parental permission, unless they are "emancipated," that is, live apart from their parents and are over eighteen. All women addicts go to Lexington. Admission to both hospitals is made by written application and is best arranged by a physician or probation officer. There is no charge for those who cannot pay. For others the fee is $9.50 a day. Every attempt is made to admit first-time patients at once, but there is usually a short waiting period for others. Inquiries should be addressed to the Medical Officer of either hospital.

The Public Health Service describes the treatment program at Lexington and Ft. Worth as aiming to prepare a patient to return home and live without using narcotics, and the first step—called withdrawal or, in some hospitals, detoxification—is to treat his physical dependence on drugs. This is accomplished by substituting methadone for heroin—or whatever other narcotic he has been using—and then gradually reducing the dosage of the substitute drug. Methadone is a synthetic drug, discovered in Germany just before or during World War II. The patient drinks the reddish colored liquid from a little glass in a ward known as "the cocktail lounge."

The withdrawal period usually lasts about four days, though it may be as long as twelve for the heavily addicted person. During this period the patient "is sick, but the decreasing doses of methadone flatten out the peaks of the illness and make it endurable. At the end he is transferred to the Orientation Ward for a convalescence period lasting about two weeks. He regains his appetite and strength during this time but shows irritability and restlessness, symptoms that may last for several more months.

"In the Orientation Ward, the patient is interviewed by members of the vocational, correctional, social service, and psychiatric staff and a course of treatment is then outlined by his administrative physician, a psychiatric resident who supervises his program until the patient is discharged.

"Fewer than a fourth of the patients get any formal psychotherapy, partly because the staff is too small and partly because many patients resist it or are judged incapable of being benefitted by it. However, all activities of the hospital are designed to have therapeutic value for people who, by and large, have never quite grown up, distrust everybody in authority (and virtually everybody else), and have substituted drug-taking for practically everything that occupies other people.

"All physically able people are assigned to jobs—in the kitchen, the butcher shop, or the bakery; as a waiter or as an attendant; in maintenance and engineering, painting and glazing, woodcrafts, needle trades, printing, or agriculture, as a laboratory assistant, an auto mechanic, an electrician, a typist or a variety of other occupations. For almost all types of work there is a training program that helps prepare the patient to get and hold a job when he is discharged. The primary purpose of the vocational program, however, is not to get patients on payrolls but to help them establish work habits and learn to put some controls on themselves and also to accept authority."

They are encouraged to take part in active sports, such as softball, basketball, boxing, and bowling, to watch TV and movies, join an orchestra, help in putting on shows, or work on the hospital newspaper, as well as to use the libraries. Protestant, Catholic, and Jewish religious services are available and chaplains offer counsel. The patients themselves form an Addicts Anonymous program similar to that of Alcoholics Anonymous. This program has been in operation since 1950, and, according to the hospital authorities, has been quite effective with many patients.

The patient should remain in the hospital at least six months. This gives him a chance to free his body of the physical craving completely and to start building a new life pattern not dependent on drugs.

The greatest weakness of the Federal hospital program is its inability to provide follow-up care when the patient leaves. As a rule, he goes back to the community where he started on the drug path, and the chances are that he will fall victim to the temptation again—and rapidly—unless family, friends, and the community extend a helping hand. The hospital authorities are the first to point this out:

"When they leave the hospital most patients need considerable help if they are to become useful citizens and assume responsibility for themselves and others. When they return to their communities, they will need help in obtaining employment and support in meeting some of the difficult problems in living they are sure to encounter. Regardless of how hard the patient has worked in the hospital, the real proving ground will be in the community to which he returns. A helping hand from the family physician, the employment agency, a probation officer, a minister, or a social worker may go a long way in determining whether the patient becomes readdicted or whether he becomes a useful and productive citizen."

In addition, about half of the patients at any given time are prisoners committed by the Federal Government, and, according to reports of ex-patients, some of the prison character remains, despite efforts of the administrators to eliminate it.

A radically new approach to the treatment of drug addiction is being taken by groups of amateurs who base their work on the philosophy of Alcoholics Anonymous that only "one who has been through it himself"—the ex-addict—can help the addict to reconstruct his personality and way of life. The best known of the institutions following this precept is Synanon, which was established in Santa Monica, California, in 1958. It is run by a remarkable ex-alcoholic, Charles Dederrich, who has fashioned a mutual-self-help organization that has already had a considerable influence on the field during its brief existence. Withdrawal is carried out "cold turkey," under the supervision of the older residents; no drugs are used to ease the process. Treatment is seen as an attack upon a character disorder, which has defied traditional psychotherapy for the most part. The Synanon staff conceives of the addict as an infant who needs bringing up in the literal sense, and they seek to teach him to become a fully responsible person, able to function as a normal adult, with adult standards of behavior. In a word, they try to help him mature. No professional therapists are used, only ex-addicts who act as "role models" and prove by their very existence and presence that rehabilitation is truly possible. Although Synanon does not release statistics, it is reported to have been able to achieve "drug-free" conditions in at least 50 percent of those who enter, and to have a comparatively low relapse rate.

Similar to Synanon is Daytop Village in New York State. This program is also based on the Alcoholics Anonymous concept, with ex-addicts as "role models," and treament is directed toward helping the addict to mature. However, there are significant differences. While the ex-addict is the heart of the Daytop program, involvement by professionals is being encouraged. Also, Daytop accepts persons committed by the courts—Synanon accepts only volunteers—and encourages young people to come in for treatment. Finally, unlike the California original, which gets no governmental or other official support but must depend on donations from interested private persons and organizations, Daytop began with a research grant from the U.S. Public Health Service and has obtained contracts from some county governments to treat addicts from those areas. Daytop's administration claims to have achieved "drug-free" results with more than 50 percent of its patients.

Adherents of the Synanon approach are impatient with the older treatment methods and insist that they are useless, pointing to the comparative success of the two new institutions in freeing addicts from drug use. On the other hand, highly experienced professionals point out that the Synanon and Daytop methods appear to be effective only for certain types of addicts and can by no means be applied to all. They argue, too, that not enough time has elapsed since the founding of Synanon for the treatment to prove itself. Nevertheless, some of the thinking and methods developed at Synanon and Daytop are beginning to affect the programs of other institutions.

The two most advanced states in the handling of narcotics problems are California and New York. In 1961, California introduced civil commitment for persons addicted to narcotics or in imminent danger of becoming addicted. Since 1959, arrested addicts have been subject to enforced treatment. The program is run by the State Department of Correction and is known as the Narcotic Treatment-Control Project. Voluntary patients and convicted addicts stay in the California Rehabilitation Center at Corona for at least six months before becoming eligible for parole as outpatients. They are kept under supervision by especially trained parole officers and given periodic Nalline tests. If they have stayed "clean" for three years, they may be discharged.

New York has adopted a similar law. As in California, an addict is committed for treatment, and the place he is to be sent and the type of therapy he is to be given is decided by a board of physicians. It is a three-year program. The new law, passed in 1966, deprives the addict of the choice he had under the former system; he no longer may decide whether he prefers treatment to imprisonment. Moreover, provision is now made for supervising his post-treatment time, and if he goes back to drugs, he is subject to commitment all over again.

The greatest immediate problem facing the administrators of the New York program is a severe shortage of facilities and trained personnel. It is estimated that there are at least 60,000 addicts in New York, perhaps twice that number (in one New York City court alone, the judge has to deal with about eighty narcotics defendents a day) and under present circumstances only a fraction of these can receive the attention and care they need. However, New York is attempting to remedy the appalling situation.

There are many experts who question the validity of any approach based on compulsion. They argue that before the addict can be rehabilitated, he must desire to be, otherwise he will resist treatment. The facts indicate, though, that the addict is often helped even if treatment begins against his will. Studies made at Lexington show that those forced to stay, as prisoners, tend to stick with treatment longer and recover. California authorities say that about 30 percent of those treated in the state's program are staying "clean." Moreover, in most cases, the nature of the drug habit rules out the voluntary approach. Usually, the addict does not want to be cured, and tends to look at a treatment center as a place where he can "clean out" when his habit has become too heavy or expensive. He seeks détoxification so that he can start all over again to build up a smaller, less expensive habit. The trouble is, that he cannot stop there. It builds again to the heavy addiction stage, because of the tolerance factor.

A completely different approach to treatment being experimented with involves the substitution of other drugs for heroin. Methadone has received the most attention. It has the ability to eliminate the craving for heroin. By taking a daily dose, the addict can, apparently, conduct a normal life and stay away from heroin. This approach is criticized by some in the field as being little more than a substitution of one kind of addiction for another. On the other hand, its adherents claim that in many cases it appears to work, that is, it permits the individual to go about his life just as the insulin shot permits the diabetes victim, and that therefore the charge of addiction is meaningless. Another drug apparently able to counter-act the craving for heroin is cyclazocine, also in the experimental stage.

In New York State, the official program recognizes that it is too early in the development of treatment methods to rest an entire program on one, and so the Commission encourages research in all that show promise. What is encouraging is that in the last few years there has been an expansion of research in the field, with developments coming rapidly in many areas. The new interest, on both the Federal and state levels, is a hopeful sign for the future.

In both the California and New York systems, it should be noted, the compulsion is aimed at total rehabilitation, not punishment. It is not a matter of throwing a person into prison, but of putting him through a long-term program of physical, psycho-therapeutic, and aftercare treatment. The aftercare part is the weakest and represents a great social challenge for the period immediately ahead.

Most of the other forty-eight states have either no programs at all for the treatment of narcotics addiction or woefully inadequate ones. In some the only facilities provided by the state governments are in mental hospitals, and often the addict is regarded as a criminal and is likely to be put in jail, where he is dealt with callously and cruelly. Very few prisons have even the facilities for administering withdrawal treatment. The addict is simply allowed to "sweat out" the physical withdrawal, without any attempt being made to alleviate his sufferings, to say nothing of providing the other help an addict needs.

A Connecticut authority on narcotics reports about the situation in his state: "There is virtually no place for the parents to turn for help. They are licked before they start. The experts are hardly that. Most narcotic experts have never even known an addict. In many cases, even the county medical officer can be of little help. Everyone turns his back on the addict—the minister, the businessman, the educator. I asked people on my staff what they would do if they found a child of theirs was an addict. Most of them answered they would just sit down and cry. All doors are closed to parents. The community must change its laws, must take a more active posture and dispense a great deal more information."

By 1968, Connecticut was reported to be planning a program to grapple with the problem.

As a rule, municipal and county governments are no better than the states in providing care for narcotics users. "I'd hate to be an addict in Chicago," says one researcher. Up to a very short time ago there were no facilities outside of prison in that great city—and it ranks number two in size of the addict population. To be an addict in Chicago has meant inevitably to tread the arrest-and-imprisonment merry-go-round, which has been so long the "junkies'" lot. By 1967–68, however, two treatment

centers had appeared: St. Leonard's House and Teen
Challenge.

The picture is slowly brightening as a result of
growing national and state awareness of the scope
of the problem and understanding of its complexities.
The passage of the Narcotic Addict Rehabilitation
Act of 1969 by the Congress is the first national rec-
ognition of the need to approach the challenge of
drug abuse from the human rather than the punitive
point of view. It provides for civil commitment. The
bill states:

> *It is the policy of the Congress that certain per-
> sons charged with or convicted of violating
> Federal criminal laws, who are determined to be
> addicted to narcotic drugs, and likely to be re-
> habilitated through treatment, should, in lieu of
> prosecution or sentencing, be civilly committed
> for confinement and treatment designed to effect
> their restoration to health, and returned to soci-
> ety as useful members. It is the further policy of
> the Congress that certain persons addicted to
> narcotic drugs who are not charged with the
> commission of any offense should be afforded
> the opportunity, through civil commitment, for
> treatment, in order that they may be rehabili-
> tated and returned to society as useful members
> and in order that society may be protected
> more effectively from crime and delinquency
> which result from narcotic addiction.*

It should be remembered, however, that there are
state laws as well as Federal covering drug abuse,
and that the state laws tend to be much harsher!

There is now being implemented a vast national

program for the creation of a countrywide network of Community Mental Health Centers, which will aim to provide a rounded service in the mental health field to communities of 75,000 to 250,000 people. The establishment of these centers is being made possible by Federal grants given under the Community Mental Health Centers Act of 1963. They may be separate buildings, or wings added to general hospitals, clinics, or other mental health facilities. The centers are to provide a range of mental health services including assistance in drug abuse cases. These centers are included in the listing of treatment facilities in Appendix A.

There has also been an auspicious growth in the number of voluntary agencies devoted to care of narcotics users. They offer a wide range of important services: detoxification, counselling, referral programs, self-help group discussion, assistance in finding work and housing, psychotherapy, pastoral counselling, and help in getting to other facilities. The agencies operate settlement houses, neighborhood centers, counselling centers, community councils, hospitals, and rehabilitation projects.

Besides the institutions run by the Federal, state, and local governments and by voluntary agencies, there are, of course, private hospitals. Not many, however, will accept narcotics cases. This is because the narcotics addict tends to be classified as requiring the kind of care given in institutions dealing with the mentally ill. The average hospital, therefore, will probably not have any facilities or staff experience in narcotics cases. Even private sanatoriums for the mentally disturbed are often loathe to accept the addict. This is because his unreliability, his tendency to think only for the moment instead of for the

future, his lying, his eternal scheming to obtain drugs
—even when he presumably wants to be cured—
make him such a difficult patient to treat.

In any case, for most people private care is out of
the question. Hospital costs are high, as are the costs
of psychiatric therapy. If the patient requires a long
stay or a long period in a sanitorium with continuing
professional help, the bill can be staggering. One
estimate for treatment over a period of a year in a
private hospital in the northeast ran to $20,000. It
can go as high as $30,000. A hospital director who
had arranged for a member of his family to obtain
treatment in a private hospital told the author that
even though he was able to get professional discounts
of considerable value, the estimate for the treatment
came to $10,000. Private psychiatric help runs from
about $15 to $60 an hour.

When the youngster is in an earlier stage of narcotics use, and indications are that only brief treatment is needed, involving, say just a few sessions
with a therapist, then you would probably be well-
advised to bear the cost of private care, if you possibly can. Although private services are by no means
necessarily better than those provided in government
institutions and by voluntary agencies, public facilities are often very crowded and you might have to
wait some time, even weeks or months, before the
youngster can be taken care of.

Most large cities and many counties have a variety
of social agencies that are prepared to help meet the
costs of private psychiatric and medical services in
narcotics cases. Your family physician will be in the
best position to know or find out which resources of
this kind are available in your community. He will

also be in the best position to make the proper arrangements.

In many areas psychiatrists, aware of the financial difficulties that people face in coping with these problems, serve on professional boards which make their services available on a low-cost or no-cost basis to families in need.

However, it should be clearly understood that many of these boards and individual psychiatrists are already overburdened. Very long waits, even for the first appointment, are the rule. Here, incidentally is another reason it is better to work through the family physician than to try to make these arrangements yourself. A social agency is more likely to accept the word of a physician than of an anxious parent who may simply be overstating the need for assistance.

But no matter what course you follow, have no illusions. However good the facilities and fine the doctors and therapists, there is no guarantee that the youngster will be permanently cured of addiction. For one thing, too little is still known about both the medical and psychological aspects of the disease. Every treatment is more or less experimental. It works in some cases and not in others. The fact is that at the present time the majority relapse, and within a comparatively short time.

The important thing for the parent, though, is not the number of failures, but the number of successes. Your youngster could be among those who do lead normal lives once they have completed the treatment. Considering the difficulties, it is encouraging, not discouraging, to know that in a survey made in the 1950's—before there were any follow-through rehabilitation programs in existence in the United

States—30 percent of those discharged from the Lexington and Ft. Worth hospitals remained free of the use of drugs during the period studied. It is also encouraging, not discouraging, to know that in another study made in the 1950's 10 percent of the dischargees from the Federal hospitals who returned to New York City, the most drug-infested city in the country, did not relapse. As noted earlier, the state of California reports that since it began its present system in 1959, 30 percent of its narcotics probationers have remained "clean," and Synanon and Daytop are reported to be achieving success with over 50 percent of those whom they accept.

The point is—there is hope. This is important not only to understand, but to believe. Belief in an ultimate cure is a critical element in treatment. The young addict senses very quickly any attitude of futility. The pessimism of parents or physicians treating him serves only to reinforce his own oppressive feeling of doom. And never forget that the wholehearted and intelligent cooperation of the family can make an enormous difference to the ultimate fate of the patient.

Moreover, as is the case with many serious diseases, a great improvement might be achieved by proper treatment even if a cure can't be. The addict can often be helped to live a relatively normal life. This is especially important in light of the fact that young narcotics users may "grow out" of their condition. It appears that as the addict matures, he settles down psychologically and has less need of the emotional crutch of the drug—or else he may have died along the way. Of course, you cannot wait for your youngster to reach his thirties or forties. He might not get there at all because of an overdose, and even if he does, so much of his life will have vanished in heart-breaking waste and misery.

There is hope—but only if you, the parent, face facts and act. The earlier the existence of the drug abuse is discovered and treatment started, the greater the hope.

12: Preventive Measures You Can Take

When all is said and done, the best way to prevent your child from ever getting involved in the narcotics tragedy is for you to *accept and act on your full responsibility as a parent.*

THIS MEANS:

- *Laying down rules of behavior to guide the youngster.*

- *Exercising discipline when called for.*

- *Establishing controls, such as curfews.*

- *Knowing where the young person is and what he is doing.*

- *Being concerned with his friends and acquaintances.*

These are not new, and they are certainly not meaningless platitudes. As Dr. Henry Brill says: "I think common sense, reasonably tempered with modern knowledge, is the answer. I do not think that the control of children has anything about it that's new. It's a problem that has existed since the beginning of time. It's written into the Ten Commandments."

An important part of your parental responsibility is making sure that your youngster is filling his time in constructive ways. You should ask yourself what kind of life your boy or girl has been leading. Has there been enough activity of which you can truly approve? Is the youngster sufficiently interested in school, sports, hobbies, extra-curricular activities? Is he or she physically and socially active? Is there normal dating? A probation officer reports that in the hard-core drug-abuse area where he works, those boys who have been active Boy Scouts have never become involved with drugs.

It is, of course, difficult for you to keep tabs on your child. If there is any ground for suspicion and if you are friendly with the parents of your child's friends, it might be a good idea for you to get together with them to discuss ways of maintaining watch discreetly and putting practical difficulties in the way of the young people who might be tempted to play with the drugs. Undoubtedly they are as worried as you are about the narcotics threat. An agreement might be worked out to set similar curfews, chaperone parties, and keep each other informed of the young people's behavior.

Keeping proper watch over your child's activities involves, of course, paying attention to his friends and what they are doing. This could lead to a rather unpleasant situation if you suspect that one of his pals is experimenting with drugs. You are concerned in the first place because if another child is infected with the drug disease, yours might become infected, too. At the same time, you undoubtedly have genuine concern for a friend of your child. What do you do?

You will have to tell his parents what you suspect. But there is danger in this. The usual response is irritation and resentment. They may be insulted and dismiss you as a busybody, or rush angrily to their child and berate him unfairly. In any case, it is possible that your child's relations with his friend—and consequently with you—will be strained. The need for tact and great care is stressed by all who have experience with such matters. A specific example of how you can handle the situation is given by Dr. Mark Kenyon. The case is you have found a box of pills in your boy's room. He denies he has been using them, says he has been holding them for his friend. Remember that your boy may not be telling the truth. The doctor's answer:

"You might call the parents and say something like, 'I found this stuff in Johnny's bureau drawer. My son tells me that he himself is not using it, that it belongs to your son. I'm concerned about the welfare of my child. I'm sure you're concerned about the welfare of your child. For this reason, I intend to follow this up by taking my boy to our family doctor to see what we should do to prevent him from becoming an addict. This is what *we* are going to do. I can only suggest that if you're as concerned with your child's welfare as I know you are, then you'll follow a similar course.' You have no way of knowing whether the other family will follow your advice, but that's all you can really do."

It may happen that your youngster comes to you and tells you that his friend is using drugs, but asks you not to tell the other parents because it will destroy his friendship, and he would never forgive you if you did. Should you risk both destroying his relationship with his friend and creating antagonism toward you by violating his confidence? Dr. Kenyon says, there is no real choice in the matter:

"Even at the risk of breaking up the boy's friendship, and depending again on how well you know the people, I would report to them what happened, but without making it a personal matter. I might say, 'My son or daughter has reported to me that some of the kids have been fooling with pills or trying marihuana. I'm concerned and I'm sure you're as concerned with your youngster as I am with mine. Since I've taken the trouble to discuss this with my child, it might be worthwhile if you talked with yours.' I would not mention that my child had mentioned theirs or any other. Now, if as a result of their own actions, those parents discover for themselves that their son is involved, then you have done something important for them, and have avoided the possible embarrassment of what they might regard as accusations."

Finally, effective prevention and your responsibility as a parent include taking community action. Sources of illicit drug supply have to be closed down and social control over the spread of the narcotics contagion strengthened. However, because of the very same fears and misunderstanding of drug addiction that make it difficult for the average family to handle its own drug-abuse problem, community action is seldom successful unless planned and carried out with great care.

For example, aroused citizens often respond to a community drug threat by calling meetings of concerned parents at which they will agree to undertake an action program. But this approach tends not to work. It is usually accompanied by an excitement close to hysteria, and is inspired by the naive belief that dramatic results can be achieved overnight. Instead, the usual result is public apathy, although there may be a brief flurry of interest aroused by newspaper stories. Even where drug abuse in a community is widespread, group action through the public meeting has tough going. Either people are just not concerned, or they are kept from attending out of fear of being suspected of harboring a drug addict at home. Moreover, committee action tends to be conducted in the glare of publicity, which in this instance can be harmful, since there is a greater chance of rash action by both citizens and public authorities.

You will find a number of useful suggestions about what to do in the following conversation on the subject held by the author with Dr. Henry Brill. Note his concern with avoiding needless publicity and public hysteria.

LAND: If you think a problem is beginning and will develop in your neighborhood unless something is done, would you get together with other parents to do something about it?

DR. BRILL: I think that group action is probably better undertaken by official, well-informed groups than by individuals.

LAND: Suppose you are just an average person. You don't know anything about official or semi-official groups. How would you get started? Would you, for example, seek help from a religious leader, or someone like him?

DR. BRILL: I think this would be my preferable

line of action. To try to channel it through some socially responsible person—the minister, the rabbi, an interested doctor in the area, the public health agency, and so forth. I would approach an institution like a department of health and ask for the person who was primarily interested in this field. I would tell him the story as a purely informational thing, and leave the wheels to turn from then on.

LAND: If you think there may be a criminal element involved, would you involve the narcotics squad?

DR. BRILL: I think that at one point I would take the local narcotics squad into my confidence. But I would do it in such a way that their hand is still free, and that they don't feel forced to take premature action. I would try to tell the story without hysteria, without excessive anxiety. I would present the facts without demanding that something be done right now to eradicate the situation, and without telling them what to do. I would see that they are informed without being forced. People forget that the kind of attitude with which they give information has a lot to do with the kind of action that public agencies take. Ill-advised action can be tripped off in a community by hysterical people. I would avoid hysteria at all costs.

LAND: What would you consider ill-advised action?

DR. BRILL: Attacks on school administration and using it as a scapegoat, mass police officers search of people in the area, or releases to newspapers of reports of drug abuse in the school.

I think that one has to take some administrative authorities into his confidence at one point. But you have to know whom you're taking into your confidence, because it is perfectly possible to become involved with someone who will handle it improperly. It has to be approached diplomatically.

LAND: Suppose you don't know who such a person is?

DR. BRILL: Then you can start out with some religious or medical advisor whom you know well. These people can lead you along the proper channels. In my experience district attorneys have been highly reliable, sensible people, who do not intend to fire prematurely or get innocent people involved. If they're approached in a reasonable way so that they are not forced to act prematurely, I think that in general these people can handle the situation well. They understand the need for respecting certain sources of information. This is part of their daily lives. *It doesn't ever have to come to an issue on the local scene. What you're working for are the behind the scenes sources of supply. You trace this three steps back and you reach the criminal element.* Incidentally, you don't have to go all the way down and get the individual experimenter. I think its terribly wrong to make an example of the individual child who has been experimenting so that he will get the feeling that he is like a carrier of smallpox. I think he needs to be helped until he is straightened out, but not to be made an example of.

There is no question that unless the local citizens supply information to the administrative authorities —and I use that term instead of law enforcement officers because there are many administrative aspects that have nothing to do with arrests—we are not going to be protected. The real trouble is lack of communication and lack of information. There is a tendency to hold back until something gross and spectacular occurs.

Even before any tangible threat has appeared in your community it is important to take preventive measures. You should encourage school boards and towns and city and county administrations to take an active interest in developing action and educational programs within the schools. You can have your club, organization, church, parent-teacher organization, social service center, mental hygiene center, and such participate.

There are some who maintain that education in this area tends to be self-defeating, that it arouses the curiosity of young people more that it deters them. The author subscribes to the position taken by the President's Advisory Commission on Narcotic and Drug Abuse, whose report was published in 1963:

> *An educational program focused on the teenager is the* sine qua non *of any program to solve the social problems of drug abuse. The teenager should be made conscious of the full range of harmful effects, physical and psychological, that narcotic and dangerous drugs can produce. He should be made aware that although the use of a drug may be a temporary means of escape from the world about him, in the long run these drugs will destroy him and all that he aspires to. The education of the teenager is, therefore, an essential aspect of any prevention program.*

As in the case of any epidemic, the sooner preventive measures are taken, the better are the chances of stopping the spread of the disease. Indeed, if there is any single point in this book to be emphasized above all others, it is that hesitation or delay in dealing with the narcotics situation can have tragic consequences. This applies at any stage of drug abuse, from the appearance of the threat to addiction. You must act decisively, but calmly and intelligently, always keeping in mind the problems and difficulties involved. Your child's life may depend upon it.

Appendix A
Where to Go for Help

Here is a list of treatment centers, hospitals, halfway houses, community health centers, State mental health offices and other places where you can get information on or assistance with drug-abuse problems.

In some instances, addresses and telephone numbers are included. To use, simply look for your State and the nearest city or town. A telephone call or letter will tell you whether the particular institution can be of help.

These agencies vary greatly in the nature of their services, and therefore, it may be necessary to call more than one to get the particular kind of assistance you require. It is usually advisable to work through your physician, your minister or some other professional, rather than attempt to make your own layman's decision as to which medical approach is best suited for your problem.

Alabama

FLORENCE
Muscle Shoals Comprehensive Mental Health Annex
to Eliza Coffee Memorial Hospital

TUSCALOOSA
State Department of Mental Health,
Bryce Hospital, Tel: 205, 758–2597

Alaska

ANCHORAGE
Division of Mental Health, Alaska Department of
Health and Welfare, 2900 Providence Ave., Tel:
907, 277–6551

Arizona

PHOENIX
St. Luke's Hospital

Jane Wyland Child Center, Inc.

St. Joseph's Hospital

Arizona Foundation for Neurology and Psychiatry
(Camelback Hospital)

Arkansas

LITTLE ROCK
Arkansas State Hospital for Mental and Nervous
Diseases (Greater Little Rock Comprehensive Mental
Center) Unit 1 and Unit 2

California

BAKERSFIELD
Kern View Hospital

BURLINGAME
Peninsula Hospital

CORONA
California Rehabilitation Center

HOLLYWOOD
Viewood Community Correctional Center, Halfway
House

LOS ANGELES
East Los Angeles Parole Community Center

Resthaven Psychiatric Hospital

Central City Community Mental Health Center

Elizabeth Fry Center, Halfway House

Economic and Youth Opportunities Agency of
Greater Los Angeles, 314 West Sixth St.

Midway Center

Parkway Center

Narcotic Addict Out Patient Program

Narcotic Prevention Project

Salvation Army Manhattan Project

Teen Challenge Center

OLIVE VIEW
Olive View Hospital

PACOIMA
Pacoima Memorial Lutheran Hospital (Golden State
Community Health Center)

REEDLEY
King's View Hospital

SACRAMENTO
State Department of Mental Health, 1500 Fifth St.
95814, Tel: 916, 445–2154

SAN DIEGO
Synanon Foundation, Inc.

SAN FRANCISCO
Synanon Foundation, Inc.

SAN JOSE
San Jose Community Mental Health Center

SANTA BARBARA
County of Santa Barbara

SANTA MONICA
Community Mental Health Center of St. John's
Hospital
Synanon Foundation, Inc.

TALMADGE
Mendocino State Hospital

VENTURA
North Coast Regional Mental Health Center

VENICE
Venice Service Center

Colorado

DENVER
Colorado Department of Institutions, 328 State Services Building 80203, Tel: 303, 222-9911

Department of Health and Hospitals, Inc. (Denver General Hospital Unit 1)

PUEBLO
Colorado State Hospital

Connecticut

BRIDGEPORT
Bridgeport Community Health Center

HARTFORD
Blue Hills Hospital

The Inn

State Department of Mental Health, State Office Building, 79 Elm St. 06115, Tel: 203, 527-6341

NEW HAVEN
Narcotics Addiction Research and Community Opportunities, Inc.

STAMFORD
Narcotics Addiction Service Center

Delaware

NEW CASTLE
Department of Mental Health, Mental Health Center of Southern New Castle County

WILMINGTON
State Department of Mental Health, Midway Professional Building, 2055 Limestone Road 19808, Tel: 302, 994–5763

District of Columbia

Drug Addiction Treatment Rehabilitation Center, 1825 13th St. N.W., Tel: 202, 462–1316

District of Columbia Public Health Department, 300 Indiana Ave., N.W. 20001 (Administering agency for rehabilitation center above)

Florida

BRADENTON
Mental Health Center of Manatee Memorial Hospital

CHATTAHOOCHEE
Division of Mental Health, Board of Commissioners of State Institutions of Florida, Florida State Hospital 32324, Tel: 904, 663–7112

DAYTONA BEACH
The Guidance Center, Inc.

Halifax District Hospital

ORLANDO
Orange Memorial Hospital Association, Inc.

WINTER HAVEN
Winter Haven Hospital

PANAMA CITY
Bay County Memorial Hospital

PENSACOLA
Escampia County Guidance Clinic, Inc.

TAMPA
St. Joseph's Hospital

Georgia

ATHENS
Athens General Hospital

MACON
Community Mental Health Center, the Macon Hospital

MILLEDGEVILLE
Central State Hospital

Hawaii

HONOLULU
The Queens Hospital

Illinois

CHICAGO
St. Leonard's House, Halfway House, 2100 Warren
Ave. 60612

Teen Challenge Center

Presbyterian St. Luke's Hospital

State Department of Mental Health, 160 North La
Salle St. 60601, Tel: 312, FI 6–2000

Indiana

INDIANAPOLIS
Marion County General Hospital

State Department of Mental Health, 1315 West
Tenth St. 46207, Tel: 317, 634–8041

Iowa

DES MOINES
Broadlawns Polk County Hospital

DUBUQUE
St. Joseph's Mercy Hospital of Dubuque

IOWA CITY
Iowa Mental Health Authority, Psychopathic Hospital, 500 Newton Road, 52240, Tel: 319, 353–3719

Kansas

HAYS
High Plains Mental Health Clinic

TOPEKA
Division of Institutional Management, State Board of Social Welfare, State Office Building 66612

Kentucky

FRANKFORT
State Department of Mental Health, P.O. Box 678 40601, Tel: 502, 564–3740

LEXINGTON
National Institute of Mental Health Clinical Research Center

Central Kentucky Regional Mental Health Board, Inc., (Comprehensive Care Center Region 10a and 10b)

MADISONVILLE
Hopkins County-Madisonville Hospital

PADUCAH
Lourdes Hospital, Inc.

Louisiana

BATON ROUGE
Louisiana Department of Hospitals, 655 North Fifth St. 70804, Tel: 504, 344–2622

NEW ORLEANS
Tulane University

Toure Infirmary

Maine

AUGUSTA
Bureau of Mental Health, State Department of Mental Health and Corrections, State Office Building 04330, Tel: 207, 623–4511

LEWISTON
Lewiston-Auburn Catholic Bureau of Social Services, (Child and Family Mental Health Center)

PORTLAND
Maine Medical Center

Maryland

BALTIMORE
State Department of Mental Hygiene, State Office
Building, 301 West Preston St. 21201, Tel: 301,
837–9000

CHEVERLY
Prince Georges General Hospital

CROWNSVILLE
Crownsville State Hospital

SILVER SPRING
Holy Cross Hospital of Silver Spring

Massachussetts

BOSTON
State Department of Mental Health, 15 Ashburton
Place 02108, Tel: 617, 227–7320

Boston State Hospital

Bridgewater State Hospital

Washington State Hospital

Massachussetts Health Center

CONCORD
Community Agencies Center

Emerson Hospital

FALL RIVER
Fall River Mental Health Center

LOWELL
Lowell Mental Health Center

Michigan

ALPENA
Northwest Michigan Child Guidance Clinic, Alpena
Area Mental Health Center

DETROIT
Synanon Foundation, Inc.

GRAND RAPIDS
Grand Rapids Child Guidance Clinic

KALAMAZOO
Borgess Hospital

LANSING
The Sisters of Mercy, St. Lawrence Hospital

Comprehensive Mental Health Center

State Department of Mental Health, Case Building
48913, Tel: 517, 373–3520

MARQUETTE
Upper Peninsula Adult Mental Health Clinic, Inc.
(Marquette Area Community Health Center)

PONTIAC
Pontiac State Hospital

Minnesota

MINNEAPOLIS
St. Barabas and Swedish Hospitals

ST. CLOUD
St. Cloud Hospital

ST. PAUL
State Department of Public Welfare, Centennial
Building 55101, Tel: 612, 221–6013

Missouri

COLUMBIA
Mid Missouri Mental Health Center

KANSAS CITY
Western Missouri Mental Health Center

Division of Mental Diseases, Missouri Department of
Public Health and Welfare, 722 Jefferson St. 65101,
Tel: 314, 635–6136

JEFFERSON CITY
Malcolm Bliss Mental Health Center

ST. LOUIS
Teen Challenge of St. Louis

Montana

WARM SPRINGS
Montana State Hospital, State Department of Mental
Hygiene 59756, Tel: 406, 442–9040

Nevada

CARSON CITY
Division of Mental Hygiene, Nevada Department of
Health and Welfare, 201 South Fall St. 89701, Tel:
702, 882–7766

New Hampshire

CONCORD
Division of Mental Health, New Hampshire Depart-
ment of Health and Welfare, 105 Pleasant St. 03301,
Tel: 603, 225–5511

HANOVER
Mary Hitchcock Memorial Hospital

New Jersey

ELIZABETH
Union County Narcotics Clinic

NEWARK
Narcotics Rehabilitation Program, 309 Washington St. 5th Floor 07102,
(For Hudson and Monmouth Counties call 201, 863–3704)

Family Services Bureau

Mt. Carmel Guild Narcotic Center

The New Will

Drug Addiction Rehabilitation Enterprise

PARAMUS
Bergen Pines County Hospital

TRENTON
Division of Mental Health and Hospitals, State Department of Institutions and Agencies, State Office Building, 135 West Hanover St. 08625, Tel: 609, 292–4242

New Jersey Rehabilitation Commission

New Mexico

ALBUQUERQUE
Vista Larga Center

New York

ALBANY
State Department of Mental Hygiene, 119 Washington Ave. 12225, Tel: 518, Gridley 4–4403

New York State Narcotic Addiction Control Commission, Executive Park South, Tel: 457–4176

BEACON
New York State Narcotic Addiction Control Commission, (Rehabilitation Center) Building No. 21, No. 13, Tel: 914, 831–4800

BUFFALO
New York State Narcotic Addiction Control Commission, Education Center, 1312 Jefferson Ave., Tel: 882–0800

Buffalo State Hospital

MIDDLETOWN
Middletown State Hospital

Long Island
CENTRAL ISLIP
Central Islip State Hospital

EAST MEADOW
Meadowbrook Hospital

WEST BRENTWOOD
Pilgrim State Hospital

WOODBURY
Nassau Center for Emotionally Disturbed Children

NEW YORK CITY

MANHATTAN
Office of the Coordinator of Addiction Programs,
250 Broadway 10007, Tel: 556–3660

Community Orientation Center, 205 West 85th St.
10024, Tel: 799–5100

Community Orientation Center—Clinton, 350 West
49th St. 10019, Tel: 582–3730

Community Orientation Center—East Harlem, 1720
Lexington Ave. 10029, Tel: 369–2727

S.P.A.N. 143 Suffolk St. 10002, Tel: 533–3560

S.P.A.N., 161 Eldrige St. 10002, Tel: 674–9120 ext.
46; 674–5563 after 6:00 and Saturday

Phoenix House, 205 West 85th St. 10024, Tel: 874–
1305

Phoenix House, 200 West 88th St. 10024, Tel: 787–
8380–1–2–3

Phoenix House, Director of Treatment Programs, 307
Second Ave. 10003, Tel: 677–2300

New York State Narcotic Addiction Control
Commission, Education Centers
    25 West 125th St. Tel: 534–2400–1

57 Columbus Ave. Tel: 799–6940–1

2127 Third Avenue, Tel: 427–6868

180 Avenue B, Tel: 673–3770

New York State Narcotic Addiction Control
Commission, Rehabilitation Centers
550 West 20th St. Tel: 929–1045

611 Edgecombe Avenue, Tel: 923–2575

550 Tenth Avenue, Tel: 565–2400

1855 Broadway, Tel: 765–0500

Addicts Rehabilitation Center

Bernstein Institute

Gracie Square Hospital

Exodus House

Greenwich House Counseling Center

Harlem Hospital

Lower Eastside Information Service Center

Manhattan State Hospital

Metropolitan Hospital

New York University Medical Center

Washington Heights Rehabilitation Center

Quaker Committee on Social Rehabilitation

The Village Haven, Inc.

West Side Rehabilitation Center

QUEENS
New York State Narcotic Addiction Control Commission Education Center, 89–08D Sutphin Blvd. Tel: 739–1130

Samaritan Day Care Unit, 130–15 89th Road, Richmond Hill 11418, Tel: 846–5200

Community Orientation Center—South Jamaica, 106–60 150th St., Jamaica 11435, Tel: 739–6006

BRONX
New York State Narcotic Addiction Control Commission, Education Center, 1363 Jerome Avenue, Tel: 588–4964

Community Orientation Center—South Bronx, 602 Bergen Avenue 10455, Tel: 635–3786

Community Orientation Center—Hunts Point, 867 Longwood Avenue 10457, Tel: 589–2726

BROOKLYN
New York State Narcotic Addiction Control Commission, Education Center, 531 Eastern Parkway, Tel: 493–6370

The Brookdale Hospital Center

Maimonides Hospital of Brooklyn
New York State Narcotic Addiction Control Commission, Rehabilitation Center, 55 Hanson Place, Tel: 875–3610

Community Orientation Center—Carroll Gardens, 482 Court St. 11231, Tel: 852–3972

Community Orientation Center—Brownsville, 579 Hopkinson Avenue 11212, Tel: 498–8008

STATEN ISLAND
Daytop Village

MARCELLUS
New York State Narcotic Addiction Control Commission, 4896 Northeast Town Line

MONTICELLO
Daytop Village

YONKERS
New York State Narcotic Addiction Control Commission, Rehabilitation Center, Sprain Road.

ROCHESTER
Rochester General Hospital
Convalescent Hospital for Children

STORMVILLE
New York State Narcotic Addiction Control Commission, Rehabilitation Center, Tel: 914, 226–9887

North Carolina

BURLINGTON
Almance County Mental Health Center

CULLOWHEE
Western Carolina College

FAYETTEVILLE
Cape Fear Valley Hospital

RALEIGH
State Department of Mental Health, 2100–C Hillsboro St. P.O. Box 10217 27607, Tel: 919, 829–7017

North Dakota

BISMARCK
Memorial Mental Health and Retardation Center

GRAND FORKS
St. Michael's Hospital

MANON
Heartview Foundation

Ohio

CINCINNATI
Child Guidance Home, Jewish Hospital,
Central Community Mental Health Center

COLUMBUS
Mount Carmel Comprehensive Mental Health Center

State Department of Mental Hygiene and Correction,
State Office Building 43215, Tel: 614, 469–2337

DAYTON
Good Samaritan Hospital

YOUNGSTOWN
Child and Adult Mental Health Center, Inc.

ZANESVILLE
Muskingum County Hospital

Oklahoma

NORMAN
Central State Griffen Memorial Hospital

Oregon

EUGENE
Sacred Heart General Hospital

PORTLAND
Raleigh Hills Sanitarium

SALEM
Oregon State Hospital (Willamette Valley Community Mental Health Center)

Division of Mental Health, Oregon State Board of
Control, State Capitol Building 97310, Tel: 503,
364–2171

WILSONVILLE
Dammasch State Hospital

Pennsylvania

BUTLER
Mental Health Guidance Clinic of Butler County

HARRISBURG
State Department of Public Welfare, Health and Welfare Building 17120, Tel: 717, 787–2600

FREDERICKSTOWN
Centerville Clinic

JOHNSTOWN
Conemaugh Valley Memorial Hospital

PHILADELPHIA
Hall-Mercer Hospital, Community Mental Health
Center

The Nazareth Hospital

Temple University Health Sciences Center

Philadelphia Psychiatric Center

Hahenmann Medical College and Hospital

Institute for Alcoholism, Narcotic Addiction and Compulsive Gambling

PITTSBURGH
University of Pittsburgh Western Psychiatric Institute and Clinic

St. Francis General Hospital and Rehabilitation Institute

REHRERSBURG
Teen Challenge

STROUDSBERG
General Hospital of Monroe County

Rhode Island

NEWPORT
Newport Hospital

PROVIDENCE
State Department of Social Welfare, 1 Washington Avenue 02905, Tel: 401, 467–7550

South Carolina

ANDERSON
Anderson Oconee-Pickens Mental Health Center

COLUMBIA
State Department of Mental Health, 2214 Bull St., 803, 758–2325

GREENVILLE
Greenville General Hospital

South Dakota

YANKTON
State Commission of Mental Health and Retardation, Yankton State Hospital 57078, Tel: 605, 665–3671

Tennessee

BRISTOL
Bristol Memorial Hospital

KNOXVILLE
Mental Health Center of Knoxville

NASHVILLE
Tennessee Department of Mental Health, 300 Cordell Hull Building 37219, Tel: 615, 741-3107

Texas

AUSTIN
State Department of Mental Health and Mental Retardation, Box S, Capital Station 78711, Tel: 512, Glendale 3–7231

DALLAS
Presbyterian Hospital of Dallas

FORT WORTH
National Institute of Mental Health Clinical Research
Center

Teen Challenge

HOUSTON
St. Joseph's Hospital, Mental Health Facility

Southmore House

Halfway House

PLAINVIEW
Plainview Hospital

SAN ANTONIO
Patrician Movement—Operation CHAPS, 1249
South St. Mary's St. 78210

Vermont

BENNINGTON
United Counseling Service of Bennington County

NEWPORT
Northeast Kingdom Mental Health Service Center

MONTPELIER
Vermont Department of Mental Health, State Office
Building 05602, Tel: 802, 223–2311

Virginia

NEWPORT NEWS
Riverside Hospital Mental Health Center

RICHMOND
State Department of Mental Hygiene and Hospitals,
P.O. Box 1797 23214, Tel: 703, Milton 4–4111

VIRGINIA BEACH
Atlantic Mental Hygiene Center

Washington

BELLINGHAM
Whatcom County Foundation for Mental Health,
Outpatient Clinic and Psychiatric Day Center

SEATTLE
King County Hospital, Harbor View Center

TACOMA
Pierce County Mental Health and Retardation Corporation

Tacoma-Pierce County Opportunity and Development Corp., P.O. Box 165 98401

West Virginia

CHARLESTON
State Department of Mental Health, 1721 Quarrier
St. 25305

ELKINS
Appalachian Community Mental Health Center

HUNTINGTON
Cabell County Comprehensive Mental Health Center,
Huntington State Hospital

Wisconsin

GREEN BAY
Brown County Hospital and Community Mental
Health Center

MADISON
State Department of Public Welfare, 1 West Wilson
St. 53702, Tel: 608, 266–2960

Puerto Rico

Centro de Investigaciones Sobre la Adicion (CISLA)

Asociacion Pro Rehabilitacion de Adictos, Inc.
(APRA)

Mayaguez Medical Center

SANTURCE
Department of Mental Health, Commonwealth of
Puerto Rico, Caguas Community Mental Health
Center

The author is indebted to the National Institute of
Mental Health, and Dr. S. B. Sells, Director of the
Institute of Behavioral Research, Texas Christian
University, for making available their latest infor-
mation on these facilities.

Because of rapid developments in the field of drug abuse, no listing can be definite or accurately up-to-date. For various reasons, any given agency may cease to function, or may drop its drug-abuse program. Should this be the case with a listing in your community, you can still obtain help by getting in touch with your county medical association who will supply information.

Appendix B
Works Consulted

AMERICAN BAR ASSOCIATION AND AMERICAN MEDICAL ASSOCIATION JOINT COMMITTEE ON NARCOTIC DRUGS. *Drug Addiction: Crime or Disease?* Interim and Final Reports. Bloomington, Indiana: Indiana University Press, 1961

ATLANTIC MONTHLY EDITORS. *The Troubled Campus.* LARNER, JEREMY. "Another Plane in Another Sphere, The College Drug Scene." New York: Little, Brown & Company, 1966.

AUSUBEL, D. P. Drug Addiction: *Physiological, Psychological and Sociological Aspects.* University of Illinois: Random House, 7th Printing, 1964.

BLUM, RICHARD. *Utopiates—The Use and Users of LSD.* New York: Atherton Press, 1964.

CASRIEL, DANIEL. *So Fair a House: The Story of Synanon.* Englewood Cliffs, New Jersey: Prentice-Hall, 1963.

CHEIN, GERARD, LEE, & ROSENFELD. *The Road to H, Narcotics Delinquency and Social Policy.* New York: Basic Books Inc., 1964.

COHEN, SYDNEY. *The Beyond Within: The LSD Story.* New York: Atheneum Books, 1966.

DUNCAN, TOMMIE L. *Understanding and Helping the Narcotic Addict, Successful Pastoral Counseling.*

Englewood Cliffs, New Jersey: Prentice-Hall, 1965.

ELDRIDGE, WILLIAM BUTLER. *Narcotics and the Law —A Critique of the American Experiment in Narcotic Drug Control.* New York: American Bar Foundation, New York University Press, 1962.

FIDDLE, SEYMOUR. *Portraits from a Shooting Gallery, Life Styles from the Drug Addict World.* New York: Harper and Row, 1967.

GOLDSTEIN, RICHARD, *1 In 7, Drugs on Campus.* New York: Walker & Company, 1966.

HARMS, ERNEST. *Drug Addiction in Youth.* London: Pergamon Press, International Series of Monographs on Child Psychiatry, 1965.

HARRIS, JOHN D. *The Junkie Priest.* New York: Coward-McCann Inc., 1964.

HESS, ALBERT G. *Chasing the Dragon—A Report on Drug Addiction In Hong Kong.* New York: The Free Press, 1965.

HOCH, PAUL H, & JOSEPH ZUBIN, Editors. *Problems of Addiction & Habituation.* New York: Grune & Stratton, 1958.

KOLB, LAWRENCE. *Drug Addiction: A Medical Problem.* Springfield, Illinois: Charles C. Thomas Publisher, 1962.

KRON, YVES J., & EDWARD M. BROWN. *Mainline to Nowhere.* Toronto: Pantheon Books, 1956.

LARNER, JEREMY, & RALPH TEFFERTELLER. *The Addict in the Street.* New York: Grove Press Inc., 1964.

LEWIN, LOUIS. *Phantastica, Narcotics & Stimulating Drugs.* New York: E. P. Dutton Inc., 1964.

LINDESMITH, ALFRED R. *The Addict And The Law.* Bloomington, Indiana: Indiana University Press, 1965.

LIVINGSTON, ROBERT B., Editor. *Narcotic Drug Addiction Problems—Proceedings of the Symposium on the History of Narcotic Drug Addiction Problems*. Bethesda, Maryland: Public Health Service Publication No. 1050, U.S. Department of Health, Education, & Welfare, March 27 & 28, 1958.

MAURER, DAVID W. & VICTOR H. VOGEL. *Narcotics & Narcotics Addiction*, 2nd edition. Springfield, Illinois: Charles C. Thomas Publisher, 1962.

MAYOR'S COMMITTEE ON MARIHUANA. *The Marihuana Problem in the City of New York. Sociological, Medical, Psychological & Pharmacological Studies*. Pennsylvania: Jaques Cattell Press, 1944.

MILLS, JAMES. *The Panic in Needle Park*. Toronto: Ambassador Books Limited, 1966.

MULCAHY, JOHN F., JR., Editor. *The Chatham Conference—Perspectives on Narcotic Addiction, September 9–11, 1963*. Chatham, Cape Cod, Massachusetts.

NYSWANDER, MARIE. *The Drug Addict as Patient*. New York: Grune and Stratton, 1956.

THE PRESIDENT'S ADVISORY COMMISSION ON NARCOTIC AND DRUG ABUSE. Washington, D.C.: U.S. Government Printing Office. November, 1963.

RUPP, ROBERT S. *Drugs and the Mind*. New York: Grove Press Inc. (Evergreen), 1957.

ST. CHARLES, ALWYN. *The Narcotic Menace*. Los Angeles, California: Borden Publishing Company, 1952.

SCHUR, EDWIN M. *Narcotic Addiction in Britain and America, the Impact of Public Policy*. Bloomington, Indiana: University of Indiana Press, 1963.

SOLOMON, DAVID, Editor. *LSD: The Consciousness-Expanding Drug*. New York: Berkley Publishing Corporation, 1966.

TAYLOR, NORMAN. *Narcotics, Nature's Dangerous Gifts*. New York: Dell Publishing Company, 1966.

TAYLOR, NORMAN BURKE. *Putnam Medical Dictionary*. New York: Putnam's Sons, 1961.

WHITE HOUSE CONFERENCE ON NARCOTIC & DRUG ABUSE. *Proceedings*. State Department Auditorium, Washington D.C.: September 27 and 28, 1962.

WILLIAMS, JOHN B., Editor. *Narcotics*. W. M. C. Brown Co., 1963.

WILLIAMS, RICHARD L., Editor. *The Drug-Takers, Time-Life Report*. New York: Time Inc., 1965.

YABLONSKY, LEWIS. *The Tunnel Back: Synanon*. New York: Macmillan Company, 1965.

Appendix C
Pamphlets, Monographs, and Reports of Particular Interest

Mechanisms of Action of Opiates and Opiate Antagonists, ABRAHAM WIKLER, M.D., Public Health Service Monograph No. 52.

Determinants for the Classification of Drug Addicts, E. PINNEY, JR., M.D., Psychiatric Consultant, Brooklyn-Cumberland Hospital.

The Mother of the Addict, PERCY MASON, M.D., Riverside Hospital.

Case Sketches, Lower East Side Information Service for Narcotic Addiction Inc. Also *Prevention of Addiction by Changing the Values of Adolescents toward Experimentation with Drugs.*

Program Description of Washington Heights Rehabilitation Center, LEON BRILL. Also *Community Approaches to the Addiction Problem and New Program for the Community Rehabilitation of Narcotic Addicts.*

Narcotics Addiction in our Community Primarily an Educational Problem. JOHN M. DORSEY, M.D., Journal of Michigan State Medical Society, May, 1961.

Poverty and Under-Education: What School & Com-

munity Can Do, WILLIAM KVARACEUS, Occupational Outlook Quarterly, Sept., 1964.

International Narcotic Enforcement Officers Association, Proceedings of the 6th Annual Conference, 1965. Also Proceedings of 5th Annual Conference, 1964, on *Non-Narcotic Drug Abuse*.

Perspectives on Narcotic Addiction. Proceedings of the Chatham Conference, by JOHN F. MULCHAY, JR.

Proceedings of Conference on Post Hospital Care and Rehabilitation of Adolescent Narcotic Addicts, Albany, 1960.

Hearings of Committees on Government Operations, U.S. Senate, 88th Congress, 1964.

Report to House Committee on Ways and Means from Subcommittee on Narcotics on the Illicit Traffic in Narcotics, Barbiturates and Amphetamines in the United States, May 10, 1965.

Exodus House: Pros and Cons of the Methadone Program, December, 1965. Also *Exodus House and Synanon, December, 1965*, *Exodus House Program for Rikers Island*, VICTOR BIONDO, *October 6, 1965* and *A Neighborhood Based Addict Rehabilitation Program*, LYNN L. HEGEMANN.

Misapprehensions about Drug Addiction, Some Origins and Repercussions, HENRY BRILL.

Note on the Many Causes of Drug Addiction, STEPHEN CHINLUND, Exodus House, 1965.

Drug Addiction, the General Problem, K. W. CHAPMAN, M.D. Federal Probation, September and December, 1956.

Hospital Treatment of the Narcotic Addict, JAMES LOWERY, M.D., Lexington.

Marihuana, a Psychiatric Study, WALTER BROMBERG,

M.D., Journal of the American Medical Association, July 1, 1939.

The Marihuana Addict in the Army, CAPTAINS MARCOVITZ and MYERS, War Medicine, December, 1944.

Cannabis Sativa in Relation to Mental Diseases and Crime in India, COLONEL SIR RAM NATH CHOPRA, Indian Journal of Medical Research.

Marihuana, the New Dangerous Drug. FREDERICK T. MERRILL—Opium Research Committee, Foreign Policy Association, Inc.

Marihuana in Latin America, the Threat It Constitutes, WOLFF, M.D. Washington Institute of Medicine, 1948.

Drug Abuse, A Manual for Law Enforcement Officers, Smith, Kline and French Laboratories, 1965.

Cyclazocine, a Long Acting Narcotic Antagonist: Its Voluntary Acceptance as a Treatment Modality by Narcotics Abusers, JEROME H. JAFFEE, M.D., LEON BRILL, in International Journal of the Addictions. January, 1956.

Narcotics Addiction: Official Actions of the American Medical Association, Department of Mental Health of the AMA, 1963.

Remarks by Louis J. Milone, Director, Nassau County Probation Department to the Task Force on Narcotics Conference, March, 1966, C. W. Post College, Brookville, N.Y.

Followup Study of Narcotic Drug Addicts Five Years After Hospitalization. DUVALL, LOCKE, & BRILL, Public Health Reports, Vol. 78, No. 3, March 1963.

Rehabilitation of the Narcotic Addict, HERBERT

RASKIN, M.D., Journal of the American Medical Association, September 21, 1964.

A Specific Approach to the Vocational Needs of Adolescent Users of Narcotics at Riverside Hospital, GOULD, SMITH & BARKER. Psychiatric Quarterly Supplement, Vol. 28, pp. 199–208, 1954.

Presenting Teen Challenge, REVEREND DAVID WILKERSON. Also *Drug Addiction Spreads Across The Nation,* The Cross and the Switchblade, Bi-Monthly Report, Teen Challenge, Inc., N.Y.

Profile Of A Narcotics Addict, YVES KRON AND EDWARD BROWN, Christianity and Crisis, Nov. 15, 1965.

Report of the State of New York Joint Legislative Committee on Narcotic Study, 1959.

United Nations Commission on Narcotic Drugs, Report of the 18th Session, Economic and Social Council, 36th Session, April–May 1963, Supplement #9. Also, Report of 19th Session, May, 1964.

Index

167

SHEFTER'S GUIDE TO BETTER COMPOSITIONS

W·0570—60¢

Although addressed to high school students, this book can also meet the needs of college freshmen and many adults who wish to review the basic principles of writing. It presents techniques tested in the classroom and stresses the *how's* of improving written expression. Numerous samples of student compositions and frequent self-testing exercises supplement the clear instructions.

SHORT CUTS TO EFFECTIVE ENGLISH

46532—60¢

Thousands of classroom and television students have used this method of learning effective English without mastering a lot of complicated grammatical rules. It's fast and easy. It will work for you. And it has a separate section of questions from typical city, state and federal civil service examinations to help you test yourself.

FASTER READING SELF-TAUGHT

W·0500—60¢

This simple five-step plan will enable you to read up to 100% faster and at the same time understand more of what you read. It can be your key not only to more knowledge and culture but also to higher pay and a better job.

6 MINUTES A DAY TO PERFECT SPELLING

75435—75¢

This book will teach you how to spell any word correctly as easily, accurately and permanently as you spell your own name.

———◆———

THE NEW MERRIAM-WEBSTER POCKET DICTIONARY

75427—75¢

Surpasses all other pocket-size dictionaries in accuracy and authority. The only pocket dictionary based on today's unabridged word authority: WEBSTER'S THIRD NEW INTERNATIONAL DICTIONARY.